Overcoming the Spirit of Offense

Overcoming the Spirit of Offense

Understanding How Offense Operates, in Order to Be Able to Overcome It

Anita McCall

OVERCOMING THE SPIRIT OF OFFENSE
UNDERSTANDING HOW OFFENSE OPERATES,
IN ORDER TO BE ABLE TO OVERCOME IT

iUniverse books may be ordered through booksellers or by contacting:

iUniverse
1663 Liberty Drive
Bloomington, IN 47403
www.iuniverse.com
1-800-Authors (1-800-288-4677)

ISBN: 978-1-5320-0691-3 (sc)
ISBN: 978-1-5320-0692-0 (e)

Library of Congress Control Number: 2016914680

Print information available on the last page.

iUniverse rev. date: 09/15/2016

I dedicate this book to my Bridegroom, Jesus, because without Him, nothing is possible. He is "the reason that I live and move and have my being."

Also, to my absolutely wonderful husband. Randy, you are such an amazing man of God, and I have such respect for you. You have always pushed us higher, and encourage all to seek deeper into the heart of God. I love the generous and giving heart that God has created in you. Thank you for 42 years of marriage and for never giving up on me.

To our amazing daughter, Abigail. You are our blessing and our fortune in this life. You have a beautiful spirit that is contagious and you are loved by all. It thrills us to see the incredible destiny and purpose that is in you. You are marked by the hand of God. Run and burn for Him everyday!

To Mary, Sandy, Phyllis and Pat, I thank you for being supportive in so many ways and for the encouragement through love and wise counsel. You helped to make this a reality!

To Mari, Tes, Sally, Danny, Pat, Beverly, Linda, Manon and Pat Shaw. Thank you so much for giving of yourselves and your time to help in proof reading. I could not have done this without you! You are an amazing blessing. Know that every heart changed and every soul that comes into the Kingdom is a result of your diligence and efforts spent in correcting my mistakes.

I am thankful to God for the honor and opportunity to witness how He is using a group of the most amazing young women of God, as you help to change the world around you.

And, to the many people, pastors, teachers, and apostles who have planted into my life, I say thank you, and the Lord bless you and keep you.

ACKNOWLEDGEMENTS

Todd White and Dan Mohler: We thank God for you both for presenting the Gospel in the purest form. Through you, we learned what Love really looks like, and how to demonstrate Love to a broken world.

Lifestyle Christianity Ministries

Bill Winston: We praise God for you for the many years that you have taught us FAITH, and how to believe God for the impossible.

Bill Winston Ministries

Bill Johnson and Bethel Church: Through your ministry we have learned that we can walk in the supernatural power of God. What a beautiful part, Bethel is to the Body. Bethel Church, Redding California

James and Beverly Rackley: Dearest friends that have never stopped reminding me that "nothing changes the Word, but the Word changes everything."

James Rackley Ministries

Kerry Kirkwood: We are thankful to God for your passion for the Word and thirst for knowledge. You continually inspire us to look deeper into the Word for the hidden jewels. We have learned so much through you and are so blessed that we can call you our friend.

Trinity Fellowship Church; Tyler, Texas

Pastor Rudy Bond: We praise God for the extraordinary passionate love that you have for people and an equal passion for the Word of God. Your passion, your enthusiasm, your love without restraint, and your humility demonstrating the Kingdom of Heaven. Thank you!

New Life Christian Church; Tyler Texas

Pastor Robert Morris: We thank you for the way that you make the Gospel simple and that you make it available to all. We are blessed by the love that you have for your people!

Gateway Church; Dallas Texas

Steven and Camilla Fulp: We are so thankful for you and the freedom of the prophetic that you seek. You see through eyes of Love, and are good shepherds to the Body of Christ. We love your hunger for righteousness.

Bethesda Church; Lindale, Texas

Steve Littlejohn: I am so grateful for the boldness that you demonstrated, when you came to me with a prophetic word. That word, so many times, has played a part in God pushing me forward. I treasure it. When I look to embrace a new season I remind myself of that word, and that God can do it because He created me to be "a strategist in the Kingdom of God!"

Tyler, Texas

There are so many, far too many, to acknowledge. Pastors, prophets, apostles, and those who walk in quiet humility who have impacted my life. You are beautiful and encouraging. I thank God for all of you and all that you have sown into the soil of my heart.

CONTENTS

PREFACE

My husband and I have a marketplace ministry. Marketplace ministry was a foreign term to me for many years, however our commitment to God operated before we understood the terminology. We love God and love people! It is impossible for one to say that he loves God, but has a problem with someone else. Our commitment to pray for people came through the love of God. For us, loving people comes before business. In doing that, God provides with abundance in the business.

We have a women's ministry, and a healing ministry that we prefer to describe as just ***being Jesus*** and doing what He would do at any given moment. Through those golden opportunities and divine appointments, we are able to love on broken ministers and their wives, apostles, prophets, and drug addicts. Men and women are broken and wounded, but there is a one common thread. That common thread is ***offense***. Every broken heart begins with offense. After many years of ministering to people and watching God heal them, we teach about the spirit of offense and how it has wrecked and ruined so many lives, wasted many years, and caused physical issues. It has been a blessing to see people healed once they realized the need to forgive their offender. This teaching bears much fruit and has changed so many lives.

God has chosen the foolish things to confound the wise. He, alone, purposed this book.

It all began as a simple outline for a meeting where I would be speaking on offense. As I was typing my notes, it began to grow far beyond the allotted time that I had to speak. I commented, the outline looked more like a book. Immediately, His response was, "It is a book!" My intentions were not to argue, but I did emphatically present my case. "I am not an author! I have never desired to be an author! I cannot do this! I am an interior designer, and that's the wrong side of the brain for this! You have chosen the wrong person! It's a crazy idea. I am not the one!"

After I finished the manuscript, I emailed it to one of my closest friends, who is a minister of over 40 years and missionary to Mexico. She and her husband, have James Rackley Ministries. She called me, and in a very loud voice said, "You did not write this book! I know you! And you did not write this!" She said, "The Holy Spirit wrote this, and it is a now word for the Body of Christ!" It was the confirmation that I needed to hear.

Once the manuscript was complete, the Holy Spirit took me to a photo of what the front cover was to be. The lioness with her face buried in the neck of the lion was what God had chosen, representing the protective heart of Jesus. It reminds us we have a place to run to when we have been offended. Wise counsel confirmed this was the photo.

The back cover photo is so special to me, for several reasons. There was an awareness in me, this was the photo for the back cover, but I couldn't tell you exactly why. All that I saw, was a bride and groom! It looked like an older groom with a younger bride, but its not so uncommon these days and set it aside.

Weeks later, I was in prayer, and I heard God say, "Did you notice that it began with a wedding and ended with a wedding?" Immediately, I knew that He was referring to the book, which was the farthest thing from my mind. As a matter of fact, I had *not* noticed that. Then He said, "and it is not a bride and groom." I hurried to find the photo. When I looked at it with new eyes, I realized that it is ***a father and a bride!*** It is a prophetic picture of the Father and the Bride of Christ, looking out into her destiny as she waits for her Bridegroom King! God is awesome and full of wonder!

We pray that you receive this from the Holy Spirit, because it is His manuscript. A **now word** for the Body. May you receive freedom when you understand that the offense that has altered your life, does not need to alter your destiny and purpose! You can be freed and healed!

Anita McCall

INTRODUCTION

Overcoming the Spirit of Offense was written by the Holy Spirit. It is the heart of God in this short remaining time to openly expose the schemes and strategies of the enemy. The spirit of offense has silently pottered generations throughout time in order to "kill, steal and destroy" their divine destiny and purpose. Being the enemy of our souls and the accuser of the brethren, the spirit of offense has been ignored, overlooked, and is the stealth instigator of all evil. Each one of us has been offended and have been left with wounds that cause us to wound others. Some of those wounds are passed from generation to generation as an inheritance of wickedness. Sliding under the radar it manifests through simple comments or opinions of men. Just **a look** can send our thought life spiraling out of control leading to unforgiveness and bitterness. Jesus warned us offenses would come. Truly it is not that the Church hasn't taught us about those scriptures. It's because taking every thought captive into the obedience of Christ has not become a revelation to our soul and the enemy of God finds a place to needle. We call it a bent place. If a tree has a limb that experiences great weight or pulling, it will begin to grow in a downward direction. When you place a heavy load on a horse, he will adjust his gait to the load he carries. By increasing the load daily will cause him to adjust his gait still more. He is being trained. One day when the load is lifted from him you will notice that his gait has not changed. His dance and spirit have been altered. People are not much different. We have been trained to be guarded, sensitive, cautious or expectant of offense. By expecting to be offended we begin to imagine our responses. The way that we see people and what we hear is filtered through the wounds of previous offenses.

We are in the last hour and it is time for the Bride to shine. The enemy of our soul has trained us to suffer repeated offense but God is lifting the skirt of the enemy to expose him so we might walk in total freedom and victory. It is time to learn how to come in the opposite spirit and love as Christ loved. "And while being reviled, He did not revile in return; while suffering, He uttered no threats, but kept entrusting Himself to Him who judges righteously;" (1 Peter 2:23)

For this Scripture to become a revelation to us we need to learn **who we are** in Christ. What does God say about who we are? More so, what does God say about the one who has offended us? The level of our understanding can be measured by how we respond after we are tested. When we begin to see how valuable the offender is to God we will walk as Jesus walked. We will see through the heart of the Father and not judge the offender. In fact, we will be able to see the offense as an indication that he is an incomplete work and God is not finished with him yet.

Overcoming the Spirit of Offense is simple and simply written. It is not written to impress anyone with biblical knowledge. However, it is designed by the Holy Spirit to expose what the enemy is doing to the Body of Christ and cause us to realize that **we** have allowed this enemy to gain ground and manifest destruction. This has been written in such a way that every person in every walk of life can comprehend. Jesus is ready for His Bride to rise up in love to defeat the enemy with a strategic maneuver called LOVE. It is time that LOVE becomes a revelational manifestation of what we should have already known. Only through a deeper intimacy with God will we be able to walk in power free from offense. Once we understand how offense has worked its schemes, we can identify the source of the offense **before** we respond.

Since He has written it, I know that God will shine a light on an area where you have been offended unaware, and He will cause you to break through into an increase of freedom that Jesus paid such a high price for.

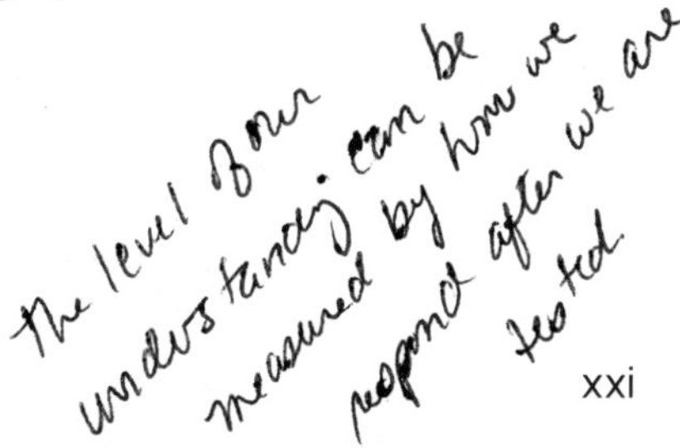

CHAPTER 1
Created to Love.

There has been a silent predator whose evil deeds have been overlooked, ignored and underestimated throughout time. Yet he leaves behind a trail of wounded hearts and broken lives. We are so used to his presence that we don't recognize him. He lurks undercover in the workplace, in the marketplace, in schools, and even in the Church. It is the **the spirit of offense**. Every crime, every broken marriage, every dissolved friendship, and every broken dream can be traced back to **offense.**

We have been offended by the silliest of things. However, some have been wounded by the cruelest of offenses. Jesus said that He came "to bring life, and life more abundantly." Each one of us has been created with a destiny and a purpose made available to us.

There is an enemy who wants to steal it from us. In order to move into your destiny and purpose you have to know the heart of God. This can only come through a relationship with Him, hearing His voice, and realizing His thoughts toward you are for good. Everyone has suffered offense. The Holy Spirit desires to shine the light on this enemy and lift the skirts on his wicked schemes.

These are the last of the Last Days and the Holy Spirit wants to shine through us so all may see His goodness. We **can** overcome the spirit of offense. In order to overcome we need to recognize who our enemy is. The spirit of offense is the bait and temptation of Satan. The Scripture speaks plainly in matters of how we are to respond when reviled, when we are talked about and when we are humiliated.

The Greek word for offense is "skandalon" (4625 Strong)-- it is a trigger or stick for bait, a trap, a snare, a stumbling block. Skandalon was the trigger of a trap on which bait was placed. When an animal touched the trigger in order to take or consume the bait, the trap would spring shut, and the animal was caught. Offense is actually, an **enticement to conduct** which will ruin the person offended.

There is an epidemic of offense, not only in the world, but among Christians. It is very important in this last hour of the Church that we are confident in **who we really are** and **what is our purpose on the earth.** Once we get a revelation of who we are, and what we were created for, our purpose becomes increasingly clear.

We were created to love.

The Church has not yet come to realize we were created to love. It's not that we haven't heard it taught but we have not had a revelation so as to walk in it. Hearing and receiving revelation are two very different things. Without revelation we continue to fall into the trap of the spirit of offense. Meanwhile Jesus is coming for a pure Bride, a selfless Bride, and a Bride who is identified as Love, and with Love, Himself.

Matthew 25:1-13 Jesus talked about ten virgins, who took their lamps out to meet the bridegroom. "Five of them were foolish, and five of them were prudent."

The definition of PRUDENT is: cautious; practically wise; careful of the consequences, measures or actions; careful to foresee the end. (Verse 3) "When the foolish took their lamps, they took no oil with them, but the prudent took oil in flasks along with their lamps. Now when the bridegroom delayed, they all got drowsy and began to sleep. But at midnight, there was a shout, 'behold the bridegroom, come out to meet him!' Then all the virgins got up and trimmed their lamps. The foolish said to the prudent, 'give us some of your oil, for our lamps are going out.' And the prudent answered 'no, there will not be enough for us and you too; go instead to the dealers and buy some for yourselves.' And while they were going away for their purchase, the bridegroom came, and those who were ready went in to the wedding feast; and the door was shut. Later the other virgins also came, saying, 'Lord, Lord, open up for us.' But he answered, 'Truly, I say to you, I do not know you.' Be on the alert then, for you do not know the day or the hour." Observe that the ten were all virgins waiting on their bridegroom.

The Church has not had the revelation that offense is one of the spirits that robs the Church of her oil. She has been distracted by so many things. Our senses have become dull and we are hard of hearing what the Spirit is saying to the Church. The lines of sin have become muddled and gray, while the spirit of offense works as a silent predator. We are skilled with creative ways to get the lost into the church but when they get there, they see the same stumbling blocks and offense they were familiar with in the world.

Matthew 18:7. Jesus said, "woe to the world because of its stumbling blocks! For it is inevitable that stumbling blocks come; but woe is that man through whom the stumbling block comes!" (Hebrew: oy 9250 an exclamation of judgement, how dreadful, cursed.)

Luke 17:1-2 "He said to His disciples, 'It is inevitable that stumbling blocks come, but woe to him through whom they come! It would be better for him if a millstone were hung around his neck and he were thrown into the sea, than that he would cause one of these little ones to stumble.'"

2 Peter 3:9-12. "The Lord is not slow about His promise, as some count slowness, but is patient toward you, not wishing for any to perish, but all to come to repentance. But the day of the Lord will come like a thief, in which the heavens will pass away with a roar and the elements will be destroyed with intense heat, and the earth and its works will be burned up. Since all these things are to be destroyed in this way, what sort of person ought you to be?"

In every area of our lives, the enemy is setting up circumstances for us to be offended. We find it in the home, marriages, the workplace and in the Church. For us to come into the fullness of our potential and fulfill our destiny, we are going to need to understand the schemes of the enemy.

We need to recognize the schemes of the enemy.

It is said that Federal agents do not learn to spot counterfeit money by studying the counterfeits. They study genuine bills until they master the look of the real thing. Then when they see the bogus money they can easily recognize the counterfeit. When in a right relationship with our Father we come to know His presence. We know true peace and joy when in His good pleasure. So much, that when the opportunity for offense is presented to us we will recognize that what we are encountering is not from the Holy Spirit. Then, we look through, to recognize the spirit that is operating through the offender, and look to see why it is there. Our assignment is to stay in communion with the Father. When I stay in sweet fellowship with Him, I will automatically begin to recognize the schemes of the enemy when under his attack. It is from this place that I can truly love the offender. For too long, we have looked at the offender as the problem. However, the source of the problem is the **thief**!

John 10:10 Jesus said, "The thief comes only to steal, and kill, and destroy. I came that they might have life, and have it abundantly."

It is vitally important through relationship with our Father that we understand who we are in Christ. We are no longer of this world. The cross of Christ has made us holy. Having been transferred from the kingdom of darkness into the Kingdom of Light, we are now children of the Most High God. A people for God to possess. Lovers that are set apart for blessing. God's plan for us is to be a witness to the nations so they can see just how good He is, and how He can take the impossible and make it glorious. As ambassadors of His Kingdom, sent to give an account of the hope that is in us, we testify of just how good God is.

When we walk in love, we are a threat to the kingdom of darkness.

With Christ in you, not walking in offense, you are a serious threat to the kingdom of darkness. The devil knows who you are and he is hoping that you never find out your potential. Satan knows that when you grasp the truth about offense you will walk in divine power. The supernatural realm will be open to you and miracles will be normal! However, if we receive the benefits of the cross but choose to walk in the deeds of darkness; the cross is of no effect for us.

1 Peter 2:9 "But you are A CHOSEN RACE, A royal PRIESTHOOD, A HOLY NATION, A PEOPLE FOR God's OWN POSSESSION, so that you may proclaim the excellencies of Him who has called you out of darkness into His marvelous light; for you once were NOT A PEOPLE, but now you are THE PEOPLE OF GOD; you had NOT RECEIVED MERCY, but now you have RECEIVED MERCY. Beloved, I urge you as aliens and strangers to abstain from fleshly lusts which wage war against the soul. Keep your behavior excellent among the Gentiles, so that in the thing in which they slander you as evildoers, they may because of your good deeds, as they observe them, glorify God in the day of visitation."

The world is looking for something real to which they can obtain hope. Peter is saying, "you are different now and you don't look like you did when you ran with people who lived in sin, being miserable and hopeless. So don't do the things that you used to do because they are watching you to see if God is really real." You can be their day of visitation. The opportunity to be offended, which was meant to derail you, can instead, become a Divine encounter with King

Jesus, if we will let grace and mercy do a more perfect work through us. God wants to allow His Love, His grace and His mercy to shine through you. So do not submit to offense! Don't take the the devil's bait!

Do not submit to offense! Don't take the devil's bait!

CHAPTER 2

What Exactly is the Spirit of Offense?

What is an offense? The definition of offense is displeasure; anger or moderate anger; scandal; a cause for stumbling; a crime; sin; act of wickedness; omission of duty; an injury; attack or assault; impediment. (Impediment is defined as anything that causes a hinderance, or obstacle applicable to any subject, physical or moral)

We are faced with opportunities everyday to respond with our opinion, have resentment or revile with anger, which can burn bridges that cause greater offense. However, when attacked, if we will come back in the opposite spirit, in love, we can change the atmosphere. If we look to see what the Father sees in the person and respond with the heart of God, we will cut off satan's scheme. Before I had an inkling of this revelation I made the mistake of separating from two different people. At the time I had two accounts that I was working on. At each job I had completed my obligations timely, and with integrity. Due to company policy I was forced to resign from one of the jobs. The other job became increasingly stressful as the client was agitated every time I saw her. Since the first was a matter of policy, I had hoped when I resigned that we would remain friends. They are so very precious and I love them. As the enemy does, once I left, he built a case against me. They were offended. We no longer see each other. A sad and grievous thing to me.

The second job was so stressful not knowing why she was angry or who she was angry with. My brother had just passed away, my mom came down with the shingles from the stress and I had an appendectomy in the same weekend. That being, the stress was so great that I felt forced to resign from that job. Neither do I see her now. She is so very precious and I enjoyed working with her.

Six months or a year later, I do not know, I attended a prophetic conference and the guest speaker came to me and said, “The Lord says, do not write anyone else off.” I knew exactly what God was talking about. I had been blessed with those jobs for divine purpose. A door was opened to me so God might demonstrate His love for them through me. I missed this opportunity because I was looking at myself and not at them. I should have given grace and opportunity to one and prayed more earnestly for the second. Friendship, fellowship and love are more important than a job, policies, or even an offense prompted by anger. Because I offended them, I no longer have the privilege to minister love to them.

John 13:34-35. "A new commandment I give to you, that you love one another, even as I have loved you, that you also love one another. By this, all men will know that you are My disciples, if you have love for one another."

Take particular notice, Jesus, Himself said two important things here. One, He said that "this is a commandment," not a suggestion or option. Two, He said we are "to love one another like He loved us." This is impossible to do without the help of the Holy Spirit and the Word of God.

Everything in this world is encouraging us to be self absorbed and self reliant, all the while the enemy of God has set snares to destroy us. And we go through our lives not understanding about the "thief who comes to kill, steal and destroy." Indeed, we have read the verse but it has not been a revelation to us. Therefore, we react and fall into the snare of offense. We never realize that we have become a puppet in the enemy's scheme.

The ultimate goal of the spirit of offense is **murder**. The enemy seeks an opportunity to gain entry through offense, in order that he can build it into unforgiveness and bitterness with the end result being murder. If the enemy cannot get you to commit physical murder, he will entice you to murder with your tongue. Character assassination. He is thrilled to have you murder their reputation, their character and their dignity.

1 John 3:15-16 "Everyone who hates his brother is a murderer, and you know that no murderer has eternal life abiding in him. We know love by this, that He laid down His life for us, and we ought to lay down our lives for the brethren."

John 15:13-14 "Greater love has no one than this, than one lay down his life for his friends. You are My friends if you do what I command you..."

The spirit of offense has been around a very long time. You must be on the alert so he does not gain an advantage. He knows exactly what buttons to push. Have you not noticed there are some things that people go through, that simply would not bother you? However, there are things that cause you to stumble where others wouldn't.

Song of Solomon 2:15. "Catch the foxes for us, the little foxes that are ruining the vineyards, while our vineyards are in blossom." This is a perfect description of our walk. Notice that the vineyard is in bloom and beginning to bear fruit, when suddenly, little foxes appear in the garden. They disrupt and begin to wreak havoc of destruction to the vineyard. The little foxes represent the small things that come to us to derail us by distracting us from our focus. They all can be powerless once Light shines on them.

Sin crouches at your door, but you must master it.

Genesis 4: Cain was offended because God did not accept his offering. God warned Cain that "sin is crouching at your door; it desires to have you, but you must master it." However, Cain submitted to the spirit of offense and murdered his brother. Cain committed a physical murder. Abel, neither offended Cain directly nor did he have anything to do with God rejecting Cain's sacrifice. It was jealousy of the relationship that Abel had with God that drove Cain to such lengths. For Cain to get to the place of murder, he meditated on **resentment**. Then, instead of mastering the enemy, which God said he could do, he chose to retaliate and and take revenge.

Many times your offender is not mad at you, he is offended at God. You happen to be a target in the vicinity where he can vent. When a person is mad at God they are blinded in seeing what they are actually doing. The only thing that they can see, is it is God's fault. They don't see that the devil threw the rock and hid his hand and God took the blame. A person who is wounded will meditate on the offense and become weak and weaker in spirit.

In the natural, the crow and the raven, which are two different birds, will locate prey that is in a state of weakness or dying. They circle that prey, watching and waiting for their chance to attack and overpower their weakened opponent. At the opportune time, they swoop in, and peck out the eyes of their victim. Indeed this a morbid thought, however, the wounded soul who has never been healed from their wounds grows weaker and weaker as they meditate on the lies of the enemy. The enemy knows and simply waits. When the opportunity is just right, he swoops in and steals the ability to **see**! No longer can the person see as they ought. The enemy steals the ability to see and brings hopelessness. Throughout Scripture God talks about being able to see and that being linked to hope. Not seeing with the natural eyes but the eyes of the spirit.

Spiritual sight is directly linked to hope.

2 Corinthians 4:18 “while we look not at the things which are seen, but at the things which are not seen...”

When a person loses his ability to see, it leaves him in darkness and torment. A dog when hit by a car, will lay on the side of the road hurting and needing rescue. It does not matter, whether it is your Pookie and you love him. In his pain he is going to bite you! People are very similar. It does not matter how close you are in relationship to a person, when they have lost their ability to see God’s goodness and love, it is very difficult to encourage them. Many times they will revile and wound the one they love the most. This is when it is important for us to be sober, alert and quick to love.

2 Kings 6:15-17 "Now when the attendant of the man of God had risen early and gone out, behold, an army with horses and chariots was circling the city. And his servant said to him, "Alas, my master! What shall we do?" So he answered, "Do not fear, for those who are with us are more than those who are with them." Then Elisha prayed and said, "O LORD, I pray, open his eyes that he may see." And the LORD opened the servant's eyes and he saw; and behold, the mountain was full of horses and chariots of fire all around Elisha."

The person who has lost the ability to see, cannot comprehend that God **will** deliver to save him. They lose sight of the revelation "greater is He that is in them, than he that's in the world." It is the greatest honor to love someone back into hope. But only if we respond in love, will we see love and hope restored. It is the kindness of God that leads us to repentance.

God is looking for those He can use, who are willing to be love so He can restore a people back to Himself. This restoration can only manifest when we are willing to "lay down our life for a friend."

CHAPTER 3

Divine Authority and Divine Purpose

The spirit of offense has an assignment whose mission is not limited by a mantle, an anointing or a spiritual calling. King Saul is a good example of that. God anointed Saul as king, until Saul disobeyed God. When Saul admitted to Samuel that he had disobeyed God, he justified his actions by saying, "it was the people." Samuel said to him, "The LORD has torn the kingdom of Israel from you today and has given it to someone else—one who is better than you. And He who is the Glory of Israel will not lie, nor will he change His mind, for He is not human that He should change His mind!" King Saul did not remain in his anointed position.

So, God sent Samuel to Jesse, to anoint one of his sons as king. God chose David, the youngest of the eight sons of Jesse.

Meanwhile, King Saul was left with his thoughts. The devil has not changed, so we can know that anger, shame, humiliation, rejection, fear of his outcome, condemnation, unforgiveness and resentment were talking to Saul. "Now the Spirit of the LORD had departed from Saul, and an evil spirit from the LORD tormented him." A servant told Saul about the son of Jesse who played a harp. The servant said, "Let them seek a man who is a skillful player on the harp; and it shall come about when the evil spirit from God is on you, that he shall play the harp with his hand, and you will be well." So, Saul sent for the harpist. Jesse sent David to the palace at Saul's request, and the scripture says that "he greatly loved David." Whenever David would play his harp, the evil spirit that tormented King Saul had to leave. Although David was brought to the palace to play for the king, he didn't stay there. David traveled back and forth from the palace to Bethlehem to tend his father's flock. He was not living in the palace as yet.

1 Samuel 17:2 "Saul and the men of Israel were gathered and camped in the valley of Elah, and drew up in battle array to encounter the Philistines." Elah means cursing; perjury. (Many times we find ourselves in the Valley of Cursing, facing what appears to be a Goliath.)

In the valley of Elah, Israel was taunted by a terrifying figure of enormous stature whose name was Goliath. Three of Jesse's older sons were there. Jesse wanted to know how the battle was going, so he sent David down with some cheese, roasted grain, and bread to give to his brothers. 1 Samuel 17:28 "Now Eliab his oldest brother heard when he (David) spoke to the men; and Eliab's anger burned against David and he said, "Why have you come down? And with whom have you left those few sheep in the wilderness? I know your insolence and the wickedness of your heart; for you have come down in order to see the battle." As you read this verse, you see years of bitterness and unforgiveness toward young David, that grew from offense; and it appears that Eliab had not dealt with it. Being familiar with Eliab's heart, David responded, "What have I done now? Was it not just a question?"

David went against Goliath with a sling and five smooth stones; killing him by a strike to the forehead. He cut off the head of Goliath, and the entire Philistine army fled.

1 Samuel 17:55-58 "Now when Saul saw David going out against the Philistine, he said to Abner the commander of the army, "Abner, whose son is this young man?" And Abner said,

"By your life, O king, I do not know." The king said, "You inquire whose son the youth is."

So when David returned from killing the Philistine, Abner took him and brought him before Saul with the Philistine's head in his hand.

Saul said to him, "Whose son are you, young man?" And David answered, "I am the son of your servant Jesse the Bethlehemite."

Note, David played in the palace on several occasions, until the evil spirit left Saul, and the Scripture says, Saul loved David. However, Saul did not recognize that it was the same young man.

Returning home from war, the women came out to meet King Saul with tambourines and dancing. 1 Samuel 18:7 "And the women sang as they played, and said, 'Saul has slain his thousands, and David his ten thousands'! Then Saul became very angry, for this saying displeased him." (He was greatly offended.)

When did Saul actually get offended? 1Samuel 15:28 "So Samuel said to him, 'The Lord has torn the kingdom of Israel from you today, and has given it to your neighbor who is better than you." This was a haunting prophetic declaration which was torment to Saul, because of his disobedience. That's quite a blow to a king's ego. 1 Samuel 18:9, "And Saul looked at David with suspicion from that day on." This offense grew and grew until Saul tried to kill David on several occasions, unsuccessfully trying to pin him to the wall with a spear.

Offense will birth a bitterness so deep, a person will hurt those closest to him. Saul's son, Jonathan did not want to believe his father was so consumed with hate nor that his father's intent was to kill David. So, Jonathan and David devised a plan to confirm David's suspicions. 1 Samuel 20:30 "Then Saul's anger burned against Jonathan", so much, that he slandered his son with cruel accusations. I Samuel 20:33, "Then Saul hurled his spear at him to strike him down, so Jonathan knew his father had decided to put David to death."

The root of bitterness manifests in retaliation and revenge.

The root of bitterness manifests in retaliation and revenge and it cannot be satisfied. It causes us to lose sight of those around us. We can no longer see anyone but ourselves. Saul was a king most offended and his anger was beyond being able to control it. When we see this type of manifestation we will find that it is rooted in offense.

Saul, later chased David from place to place, trying earnestly to kill him. Have you ever felt like someone was relentlessly trying to destroy you?

David refused to harm Saul, even though the men around him were telling him it was the very thing that he should do. (The devil is a liar, and will even resort to using the prophetic word or scripture.) 1 Samuel 24:4 "and the men of David said to him, "Behold, this is the day of which the Lord said to you, 'Behold I am about to give your enemy into your a hand, and you shall do to him as it seems good to you.'"

Away from their homes and their families and without rest, David's men had been on the run with him from place to place for quite a while.

Proverbs 14:12 "There is a way which seems right to a man, But its end is the way of death." Whether it was out of weariness or offense for David, the eyes of David's men were blinded to seeing Saul's value and his position as king. David was in the cave when Saul came in to relieve himself. (1Samuel 24:3-6) David, who happened to be in the cave, secretly took opportunity and cut off the hem of Saul's robe, but afterwards David's conscience bothered him. He repented before his men and said to them, "Far be it from me, because of the Lord, that I should do this thing to my lord, the Lord's anointed, to stretch out my hand against him, since he is the Lord's anointed." And David persuaded his men with these words and did not allow them to rise up against King Saul. And Saul arose, left the cave, and went on his way."

David already knew he was anointed to be king and it was God, who had chosen him. However, David still honored Saul and his anointing and he waited for God to vindicate him. He did not try to vindicate himself. David had a clear revelation of respect and honor to authority. When we are offended we want to be vindicated! We often don't want to wait for God to do it and so, we will listen to the words of the enemy who pushes us to revile and retaliate.

In 1 Samuel 26, Saul was camping in the hill of Hachilah, and his personal mission was to find David and kill him. David and Abishai crept into Saul's camp at night, and Abishai said to David, "Today, God has delivered your enemy into your hand; now therefore, please let me strike him with the spear to the ground with one stroke, and I will not strike him the second time." But David said to Abishai, "do not destroy him, for who can stretch out his hand against the Lord's anointed, and be without guilt?" David also said, "As the Lord lives, surely the Lord will strike him, or his day will come that he dies, or he will go into down into battle and perish. The Lord forbid, that I should stretch out my hand against the Lord's anointed; but now please take the spear that is at his head and the jug of water, and let's go."

Intimacy with our Father causes us to be able to love.

David had the heart of God and was able to stand against offense, even in these extreme situations. He knew God through his personal relationship with Him. It is going to be through intimacy with our Father, if we are to be able to love and honor others while they are reviling against us. David bore witness to Saul's value and his anointing. God called David, "a man after his own heart." After removing Saul, God made David their king.

1 Samuel 13:14 Samuel talking to Saul, said, "But now your kingdom shall not endure. The Lord has sought out for Himself a man after

His own heart, and the Lord has appointed him as ruler over His own people, because you have not kept what the Lord has commanded you."

King Saul's bitterness and hatred that began with unintended offense ended in the death of Jonathan and his other sons. He, then committed suicide.

The Bible is full of intrigue as God reveals the lives of real people with real blunders and mess ups. We wonder what happened to Eliab? How did he end?

Who is the Lord's anointed that God has placed in your life? Whether it is your husband, your father, your pastor, your employer, your supervisor, these are governing authorities that are anointed by God and placed in your life for a **purpose**.

1 Peter 2:13-15 "Submit yourselves for the Lord's sake to every human institution, whether to a king as the one in authority, or to governors as sent by him for the punishment of evildoers and the praise of those who do right. For such is the will of God that by doing right you may silence the ignorance of foolish men."

Romans 13:1 "Every person is to be in subjection to the governing authorities. For there is no authority except from God, and those which exist are established by God."

That does not mean you submit to them in sin, it means that you love them and honor them for their value regardless of their sin.

Romans 13:8 "Owe nothing to anyone except to love one another; for he who loves his neighbor has fulfilled the law. For this, "YOU SHALL NOT COMMIT ADULTERY, YOU SHALL NOT MURDER, YOU SHALL NOT STEAL, YOU SHALL NOT COVET," and if there is any other commandment, it is summed up in this saying, "YOU SHALL LOVE YOUR NEIGHBOR AS YOURSELF."

God has placed people in authority over you who are anointed and divinely placed there with **purpose**. I know a young woman that came for prayer. She said, "please pray that God will give me another job. My boss is mean and degrading, and I have been asking God to 'get me out of here!' He has not answered me, and I am so miserable. My boss makes me feel like I can't do anything right. He talks down to me." I told her that she was in boot camp, and once she learned to see him as God sees him and love him, then she could expect advancement. We prayed, asking God to do the work in her first. Being eager to get out of there and be promoted by God, she was determined to see his value from her heart. She began to speak life into him, encouraging him, and even would occasionally bring him a snack. Her heart began to change in this process. He allowed her to pray for him, and he would never have allowed that before. Soon, he began to see her differently. His tone mellowed. She began to enjoy work, and she was no longer being offended. He was seeing Christ in her and was becoming hungry to hear more about her God. Before the year was up, instead of leaving for another job, he sold his business to her and retired. They parted as good friends. Needless to say, it was a miracle from God! It was a miracle that he sold the business to her, but God also provided the financial miracle she needed. God's favor was poured out on her because she chose to love instead of revile. You could be missing your divine opportunity for advancement. But, because you are allowing the spirit of offense to minister, you lose sight of your purpose.

Proverbs 27:17 "Iron sharpens iron, So one man sharpens another."

CHAPTER 4

Hope Has a Name.

These stories are so very important to us today because they are the footprints of those who have have traveled before us. 1 Corinthians 10:11 “Now these things happened to them as an example, and they were written for our instruction, upon whom the end of the ages have come.”

Romans 15:4 “For whatever was written in earlier times was written for our instruction, that through perseverance and the encouragement of the Scriptures, we might have hope.”

Paul adds, “now may the God who gives perseverance and encouragement grant you to be of the SAME MIND WITH ONE ANOTHER according to Christ Jesus.”

Colossians 4:6 "Let your speech always be with grace, seasoned, as it were, with salt, so that you may know how you should respond to each person." We are the salt God uses to make the world thirsty. At the same time, when we respond in love, we are the salt that will help a wound to heal. The world is in despair and hopelessness. There is no peace and no joy. Someone in the course of their life has wounded them. Through the wound of offense, they have lost their hope. They try to suppress the pain with whatever temporary fix they can get. It can be drugs, sex, alcohol, food, shopping or money. However, when they see someone who truly has joy and peace, who returns with love, in spite of what has been done to them, it makes them thirsty for God. We have the grace made available to us to give hope where it has been stolen. Everything that we need to be able to walk in righteousness has already been made available to us. We are a testimony for someone else. We carry Hope inside of us. And Hope has a name! His name is Jesus!

We are a testimony of Hope for others.

2 Peter 1:2-4 "Grace and peace be multiplied to you in the knowledge of God and of Jesus our Lord; seeing that His divine power has granted to us everything pertaining to life and godliness, through the true knowledge of Him who called us by His own glory and excellence. For by these He has granted to us His precious and

magnificent promises, in order that by them, you may become partakers of the divine nature, having escaped the corruption that is in the world by lust."

Romans 12:10 "Be devoted to one another in brotherly love, give preference to one another in honor."

Throughout scripture we see the spirit of offense in operation. We see those who did not "run well". However, we see those who ran well and did not succumb to the spirit of offense, but instead changed the course of events for many generations. Likewise, we have seen the devastation linked to those who did not run well but left generations scarred and imprisoned by their deeds. Many laws have been passed as a result of individuals and nations who have been devastated by the sins of abuse. Prisons house talented people who had destiny and purpose inside of them, but are there as victims of perpetual offense.

The enemy uses a multitude of ways to tempt us with the spirit of offense and his bag of tricks seem endless. All are attached to a previously rooted wound and manifest differently for us all.

"They didn't speak to me."
"I was looked over, and I deserved that promotion!"
"They saw that I was waiting for that parking space."
"He accused me of something that I didn't even do."

"They didn't invite me to the meeting."

"I was left completely out of the conversation."

"She gave Sue a gift for her birthday, but she didn't even acknowledge my birthday."

"He answered me rudely and abruptly."

"They acted like I was invisible and not even around."

"She never paid me the 5.00 that she owed me."

"They didn't even say 'thank you'."

"He never once apologized for what they did to me."

"She never bothers to call me."

"Did you hear what she said to me!"

The temptation to be offended is never ending. Even though opportunities are limitless, the spirit of offense is a trespasser and is not suppose to be in the Body of Christ. When God is not the source of our expectation, we will end in frustration and offense. We are offended because our expectations are not met. The spirit of offense steals our joy and peace. The strategy of the enemy is to apply enough pressure, he can get you to make a choice to move outside of love. However, every time that you choose love instead of choosing resentment and reviling, you get promoted! You get blessed! Not only does the window of Heaven open to pour out a blessing on you, but it leaves a mark on the life of the offender as testimony of the Father's heart. You get stronger and stronger! And they get a glimpse of the Father's love.

Ephesians 4:32 "And be kind to one another, tender-hearted, forgiving each other, just as God in Christ also has forgiven you."

How we respond makes all the difference.

An offense can be awkward and it can be humiliating. However, it is how you respond that makes the difference.

There was a visiting minister that came to our church one Sunday. The word that she gave so deeply touched my heart. It was one of those messages that was a spiritual surgery and healing all at once. After the service, I wanted just to say "Thank you for being obedient to speak truth in such love." Just to the side of the platform was a small room, which I have now come to learn as the 'green room'. The door was open, and I heard laughter and voices. However, I was taught as a child you always knock, even if the door is open. I knocked and two voices said, "come in." When I stepped inside the small room, there sat three women, the pastor's wife, the visiting minister and another evangelist within the church. They stared without saying a word. It was incredibly awkward and it felt as if we were all naked and speechless. It was as if time stood still and a moment seemed like an hour. I spoke up and said, "I wanted to thank you for the amazing message that you just taught. I was so blessed by it." They stared at me without a word. I felt as if I had just crossed the no fly zone, forbidden territory. I responded to the awkward moment with a “that’s all I wanted to say.” I turned to leave and they went back into their conversation without ever speaking a word to me. Although there was no sign which read Green Room, Private or No Admittance, there must have been an unwritten rule that everyone knew but myself. It was a snare set up to steal the seed that had been planted during the message. And it was my first experience with elitism in the church. The enemy knew what he was doing. It wasn’t them, it was him.

The church has not taught about the spirit of offense and there are similar instances that go on every day. However, we are without excuse. Because although the church hasn’t taught about the spirit of offense, the scripture does. The offense that I described, left me humiliated and feeling like an outsider. As if I had no value. I didn’t know how to process all of it. I went straight from there to the car where my family was waiting on me. My husband sensed something and asked “what’s wrong?” I told him and then, we were both offended. Offense is designed to cause invisible barriers which will quench the love of the brethren. I had to take the Word of God and allow the Holy Spirit to wash me, and remove any shame and humiliation that I felt, so that I could bless them from a pure heart. I don’t believe that they would have purposely done anything to cause me to stumble but there is a devil that would. This is shared as an example. However, as this is written, the enemy reminds me of exactly how that felt. The sting of it all. Even now, I must stand on guard not to take the bait. He will bring back to us, those feelings that we felt. He can play the movie over again and cause you to feel those same blushing feelings. We can see it all over again, in detail. If we have asked for forgiveness from Father God for taking offense, and have forgiven them, then it's OVER! It's gone! The reason the enemy will bring back the memories, and play those old movies in your mind, is to get you to revisit those situations in your thoughts. This is not from the Spirit of God. It is the enemy. The spirit of offense is bringing it all back to see if we will take his bait.

1 Peter 5:8-9 "Be of sober spirit, be on the alert. Your adversary, the devil, prowls around like a roaring lion, seeking someone to devour. But resist him, firm in your faith, knowing that the same experiences of suffering are being accomplished by your brethren who are in the world."

The spirit of offense welcomes your attention. Don't go there. If you have repented for being offended, don't go back there! It's deadly! Focus on Jesus, and bless the offender.

Luke 6:27-28 "But I say to you who hear, love your enemies, do good to those who hate you, bless those who curse you, pray for those who mistreat you."

Forgiveness is not an option,
it is a commandment.

If you have unforgiveness towards anyone, it is a prison. Even if someone were to be offended for you, they can never feel what **you** feel. It's your prison. Forgiveness is not an option. It's a requirement. I had to lay my Green Room experience down at my Fathers' feet, and forgive so I could move on. If you refuse to forgive, you **will** stay right in that place of quick sand where you will continue to sink, until you are no longer fruitful for any good work. You will have lost your ability to **see**.

James 5:8-9 "You, too, be patient; strengthen your hearts, for the coming of the Lord is at hand. Do not complain, brethren, against one another, that you yourselves may not be judged; behold, the Judge is standing right at the door."

This is a very significant verse. When we choose not to forgive, we actually have complaint against one another. The first important thing to note is that, when you do complain, you will be judged. Second important thing to note is that "the Judge stands right at the door." A doorway is a transition or a threshold, which separates you from where you are, to where you want to go. If you are outside the house, for you to go inside the house you have to go through the door. If the Judge is standing at the door, I guarantee you, you cannot get past Him. You cannot make advancement in the Kingdom of God when you have a complaint against your brother and are judging him.

It does not matter what **he** has done. It does matter, however, how **we** respond to him.

John 15:13 "Greater love has no one than this, that one lay down his life for his friends."

Matthew 6:14 "For if you forgive men for their transgressions, your Heavenly Father will also forgive you."

1 Corinthians 13:5 "love does not take into account a wrong suffered...." This description of Love, indicates that there are repeated opportunities of offense because it uses the word account. However, we are not to take account of them. Account means 'to keep a record of'. Keeping record or account, is the incubating tank where bitterness is growing. The saying, "I will forgive them, but I won't forget", is a mindset with a determination to keep record of the offense. To forgive requires making a choice to give it up completely. The Greek word for forgive is aphesis, and it means 'deliverance, pardon, complete forgiveness, a sending away, a letting go, a release'. A complete forgiveness, in short, means to treat the offense as if it never happened. God said our sins are separated as far as east is to west. What if God were to say, "That's it! I am done! I will forgive her, but I won't forget it!" Sounds ridiculous! If it sounds ridiculous and if we can't see God saying those things, then it shouldn't come out of our mouths either. We have heard people

say, "I will forgive her one more time, but this is her last chance." What about when Peter came to Jesus with questions of limiting opportunities for forgiveness?

Forgiveness is the key that locks the door to resentment and retribution.

Matthew 18:21-22 "Then Peter came and said to Him, "Lord, how often shall my brother sin against me, and I forgive him? Up to seven times? Jesus said to him, "I do not say to you, up to seven times: but up to seventy times seven." Jesus was saying, "Don't stop! Continue to forgive!"

Matthew 6:14-15 "For if you forgive men for their transgressions, your heavenly Father will also forgive you. But if you do not forgive men, then your Father will not forgive your transgressions." Forgiveness is a commandment. If we are honest with ourselves, we have thoughtlessly, and even intentionally offended others. Love is seeing the need to forgive, pardoning the offender, seeking restoration, and allowing the Holy Spirit to remove the awareness of the offense. Flesh will always say, "it was their fault, not mine!" Or, "I wouldn't have said that, if they had not said what they did!" But Paul wrote in First Corinthians 6:7, "why not rather be wronged? Why not rather be defrauded?" This cannot be done without a relationship with the Father, desiring to please Him and allowing our flesh to die. Flesh wants to demand its rights and believe that retribution is justified. But in the Kingdom this is not so.

Forgiveness is the key that locks the door to resentment and retribution.

Flesh wants to demand its rights.

CHAPTER 5

Love Never Fails.

1 Corinthians 13 is known as the Love Chapter. It describes what love is and what love is not. We can do all the right things with the wrong motives and it profits us nothing.

"If I speak with the tongues of men or of angels, but do not have love, I have become a noisy gong or a clanging cymbal. And if I have the gift of prophecy and know all mysteries and all knowledge; and if I have all faith, so as to remove mountains, but do not have love, I am nothing. And if I give my possessions to feed the poor and deliver my body to be burned, but do not have love, it profits me nothing. Love is patient, love is kind, and is not jealous, love does not brag, and is not arrogant, does not act unbecomingly; does not seek its own, is not provoked, does not take into account a wrong suffered, does

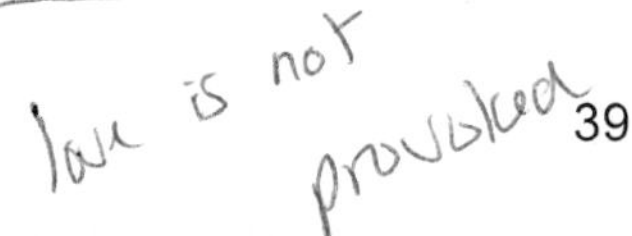

not rejoice in unrighteousness, but rejoices with the truth; bears all things, believes all things, hopes all things, and endures all things. Love never fails...."

Love looks into the heart of the offender.

No, love never fails. It's the gift that never stops giving. Love does not walk in offense. Love looks into the heart of the offender and sees an opportunity to demonstrate the heart of the Father. We are born again so we might be living epistles, to be read by all men, as a love letter from the Son of God, who loves them intensely. When we choose to love instead of reviling back, we gain an advantage over the enemy.

I met a young lady who came to me for prayer. She said, "Would you pray for me? My dad and I have been at odds lately. He is drinking a lot." I could see her heart was grieved about it, and I could see the love and concern that she had for her dad. So we prayed for her daddy, and asked the Holy Spirit to give her creative ideas how she might show her dad just how special and important he is. We did not focus on his drinking or the arguing, but instead, we blessed her father and their relationship. She began by sending him a text the next day, telling him how much she loved him, and how he had blessed his family. Then she told him how much they appreciated all that he did for them. That night, she was sitting on the sofa, and he came in and sat next to her. He told her how much the text meant to him. He said, "Thank you. That really made my day!" Every chance she got, she did something to show her love. She made his favorite dessert, put a card where he could find it. Soon she noticed that he wasn't drinking as much. Excited, she called to say, "Ms Anita! It's working! We are getting along and he does not drink as much! We are eating together like a real family!" The next week, she called to say, "Ms Anita, my dad went to church with us for the first time ever! God is working!" A couple of weeks went by, when I received another call. She said, "I have to tell you this! Saturday morning, my dad said, 'You used to make pancakes for us on Saturdays. Would you make pancakes this morning?' I told him yes, and I went to the grocery store and purchased what was needed and came back and made pancakes. We sat down to eat, and my little sister said to me, you go to church, shouldn't you say a prayer"? My dad, said, "No, I want to say the prayer." Then she said, "Oh, Ms Anita, he said the most beautiful prayer!"

This is what our God can do, when we look past what someone is doing and choose to love them instead. This is the perfect example of what happens when we show someone we see the value in them, and are grateful for them. The story is not over for this family. The father is now going to church and seeking the Lord. It all happened when a daughter chose to love her dad, and helped him to see his value.

Offense comes, and then, the opportunity for a response. First, the spirit of **resentment** ministers, then the spirit of **retaliation**, and next the spirit of **revenge**. Our natural fleshly instincts are to hit back. If you have watched children, you see reactions in the simplest and immature form. One child may immediately hit back, while another may run off to pout, but the end result of the enemies' schemes is the same. The one who ran off, will sit and meditate on the offense. That is the precise place where the enemy builds. In our thought life.

Proverbs 25:28 "Like a city that is broken into and without walls, is a man who has no control over his spirit." The walls of the city kept the enemy out so the residents could live in peace, and not be pillaged and destroyed. The writer of Proverbs is describing a man that does discipline his thought life, his mind. Because he does not discipline his thought life, the thief can come to plunder and carry off his goods. His health, his relationships, his finances, and lastly, his ability to see.

Ephesians 6:12 "For our struggle is not against flesh and blood, but against the rulers, against the powers, against the world forces of this darkness, against the spiritual forces of wickedness in the heavenly places." Our fight is not against the offender. The fight is against the one who uses and influences the offender.

James 1:2-5 "Consider it all joy, my brethren, when you encounter various trials, knowing that the testing of your faith produces endurance. And let endurance have its perfect work, that you may be perfect and complete, lacking in nothing. But if any of you lacks wisdom, let him ask of God, who gives to all generously and without reproach, and it will be given to him."

The level of your understanding can be measured by how you respond.

The spirit of offense seeks to steal your destiny and purpose by keeping you from becoming a mature man. It comes to test your faith. Do you really believe in LOVE? The level of your understanding can be measured by how you respond after you are tested. The spirit of offense comes to squeeze you to see what areas are still alive. The real test of your faith is not always about how you responded, but what did you do after the response? Did you run to Father? Was there sorrow and repentance? Or, did you choose to retaliate and hold a grudge? Did you mediate on the offense for days? Did you look for someone to side with you in your offended state? "When you got squeezed, what came out?" I heard this perfect analogy. When you squeeze oranges into a glass, it should not taste like apple juice. It should be orange juice. Why is it when a Christian gets squeezed by the devil, everything but Jesus comes out?

A mature man returns with a response in the opposite spirit. The opposite spirit is love.

To "consider it all joy" is the fruit of the revelation that "love covers a multitude of sins." If I Peter 4:8 is not a revelation to you, you will not be able to manifest the fruit of compassion.

My husband and I have a business. When we were just getting started, the smallest sale was greatly appreciated. One day, a pastor in the community came in to buy a gift for his daughter's birthday. We sold him a jewelry box with the understanding that he would bring the payment in a few days. He did not come with the money. Many months went by and he avoided us as much as possible. My husband really struggled with the behavior. He would say, "This is a man of God." On occasions, we would see him eating out with his wife and he would always say, "I am going to pay you." He didn't. My husband would see him and say, "But, he is a pastor!" It was torment for my husband because my husband is a man of righteousness, and did not have a grid for that kind of behavior. One day we happened to be at a reception and the pastor was there. My husband went over to him, asking if he might speak with him. He told him "by not paying his debt, he had actually stolen it." For my husband to have peace from the injustice, he would have to release the man and forgive the debt. Randy forgave him, and the enemy was no longer able to torment my husband with the offense. He released and blessed the man, and left him sitting there speechless. (He never paid the debt, but my husband was free.)

1 Peter 4:8 "Above all, keep fervent in your love for one another, because love covers a multitude of sins."

Romans 12:21 "Do not be overcome by evil, but overcome evil with good."

We must remember that the offender is not the enemy.

In order to love the person that is offensive, we must realize they are not the enemy. That is foremost. The spirit of offense seeks to ruin and is the **thief** that Jesus spoke of. Whatever we submit to, will rule over us, and whatever we judge, we will become like. If you are offended by your parent and you have judged them, you can be assured that there will be a day that you will be just like them.

John 10:10 Jesus said, "the enemy comes but to steal, kill, and destroy; I came that they might have life, and might have it abundantly." The word "abundantly" in the Greek is perissos, and it means 'greater, excessive, exceedingly, beyond what is anticipated, exceeding expectations, going past the expected limit, more than enough'. Why wouldn't a thief want to steal our abundance! The devil looks to steal your peace, your joy and gladness, your strength, your wisdom and your relationship with the Father.

The word "kill" means to 'put an end to'. If the devil can trap us into relying on our emotions, he can kill our finances, our relationships with friends and family, our job, our health and thereby kill our destiny, purpose and calling. He can cause us to make huge mistakes that will derail our purpose in life and those around us.

The enemy will foster unforgiveness into roots of bitterness. Hebrews 12:15 "See to it that no one comes short of the grace of God; that no root of bitterness springing up causes trouble, and by it many be defiled." Apostle Paul is speaking to the Church, not to unbelievers. "See to it" means to be careful, and certain. It also means, "do whatever is necessary to get the results needed." To come 'short' means 'to fail to meet a goal or standard'. The grace of God is the power to overcome sin and is there to help you to overcome offense.

Titus 2:11-12 "For the grace of God has appeared, bringing salvation to all men, instructing us to deny ungodliness and worldly desires and to live sensibly, righteously and godly in the present age,..."

I Corinthians 10:13 "No temptation has overtaken you but such as is common to man; and God is faithful, who will not allow you to be tempted beyond what you are able, but with the temptation will provide the way of escape also, that you may be able to endure it." When we fall into the trap of the spirit of offense, the grace of God is there for us, to help us escape the snare of the devil **before** resentment builds its case. Once resentment builds its case against the person who has offended you, retaliation and revenge begin to work. However, the Holy Spirit is there to help us and deliver us.

James 4:7 "Submit therefore to God. Resist the devil, and he will flee from you." The Greek word for 'submit' is hupotasso. It means to place or rank under; subject to; to put under subjection to the will of another; to obey. As a child of God, it is our desire that "His will override our will." When we say, "Father, what is Your will in this?" His answer will always be LOVE. Being fully submitted to God, means you no longer have opinions. You, no longer, decide if you want to love. When you are deeply in love with your Father, your desires are automatically aligned with His will.

His answer will always be love.

This is where you **be** like Jesus and love the offender. In the midst of the fire, when you choose to love instead of resenting what they said, you "are submitting to God, and resisting the devil." The verse says that (as a result), "the devil will flee." He cannot operate where submission to God is working. He will give up, leave and return at an opportune time to see if you are of the same mind. God simply wants you to give up what you were never created to be. You were created to be Love and bring joy to your Father. You were never created for you! You were created for His good pleasure. In His good pleasure is **the blessing.** In the blessing, are all the blessings and the fullness thereof. You were not created for destruction, you were created for greatness. Greatness lives inside of you. And, Greatness has a name! Jesus!

Psalms 91:2-4 "...I will say to the LORD, "My refuge and my fortress, My God, in whom I trust!" For it is He who delivers you from the snare of the trapper and from the deadly pestilence."

He will cover you with His pinions, and under His wings you may seek refuge; His faithfulness is a shield and bulwark...." That verse describes a trapper and a snare. When we submit to God, it is He, who delivers you from the trap that the enemy has set to destroy you. However, it is up to you to be able to recognize the snare. The trap will not close until you take the bait.

The strategy of satan is to destroy you and take as many with you as he possibly can. He seeks to reproduce an offspring who looks, sounds, and behaves just like him.

John 8:44 "You are of your father the devil, and you want to do the desires of your father. He was a murderer from the beginning and does not stand in the truth because there is no truth in him. Whenever he speaks a lie, he speaks from his own nature, for he is a liar and the father of lies". The enemy is seeking to father a generation. If he can father a generation, he will create a culture destined for death. Sadly he has wreaked havoc in the Body of Christ. Those who are called to be a standard of Love and a light set on a lamp stand. All the while the world is waiting to see **something that works!**

CHAPTER 6

Guard Against Unforgiveness.

Our actions will pinpoint any unforgiveness residing in our heart. When we find ourselves avoiding people when we see them, or we experience a negative emotion rising up in us, we can know we have received offense through them. If you cannot say you have a desire to see them blessed as much you want to be blessed, then you can ascertain you have not yet fully forgiven them.

When we hear something unfortunate has happened to them, is there a thought that says, "well, she deserves whatever she gets." Or, "I am not surprised." Or, "I knew that would happen to her." What about just a tinge of pleasure? If there is a wall of separation, we can know that we have unforgiveness. True forgiveness wants the best for them. These are our measuring tools.

Matthew 22:38-39 "This is the great and foremost commandment. The second is like it, 'YOU SHALL LOVE YOUR NEIGHBOR AS YOURSELF."

True undefiled love says, "allow them to be served first."

We all desire good things for ourselves and we want to see the blessing and favor of God be on our lives. However, can we say that we want to see God shower the one who offended us with the same amount of favor? True undefiled love says, "allow them to be served first." When our heart feels this way, then we can know we have truly forgiven them.

The word 'neighbor', "plésion", does not apply only to people who live in our vicinity of residence. It is not geographically placed individual. The word 'neighbor' applies to a neighbor, a friend, a companion. But, it also can be a perfect stranger. The cashier at the grocery store, a co-worker, or the person who just pushed in front of you in line, is your neighbor.

1 John 4:20 "If someone says, "I love God," and hates his brother, he is a liar; for the one who does not love his brother whom he has seen, cannot love God whom he has not seen."

If we cannot love the person at the register because they were rude, how can we love God whom we cannot see. The problem in the Body of Christ, is we do not have a revelation of what the Father sees.

I had to pick up some things at the store one day. As I walked up to the register to check out, the cashier looked as if she wished that I had gone to the register beside her. Her countenance said the best thing for her, would be that I disappear completely. I placed my purchases on the belt and pulled out my most cheerful voice. Trying to make conversation, I made a comment about "what a gorgeous day it was", and then, "how lovely her hair looked." She scanned without a word, and tried with concerted effort not to make eye contact. It was the perfect opportunity to be offended. I could have said things like "I believe someone needs to work on their customer service skills!" Or, "Isn't it your job to be polite?" Or, "Wow! You really have the attitude going on!" So many fiery darts were assailing my mind. I leaned into the Holy Spirit to ask, "Father, show me what you see about this young lady. I know you love her, and I am asking you to help me love her too, so I can be a blessing in her day." As she turned to put my things into a bag, I noticed the name on her name tag was Geneva. I commented, "What a beautiful name, Geneva! It suits you! You are a such a lovely girl and I can see you are hurting. I am going to pray for you today." She responded, "Thank you. My mother is in the hospital and when I was going to see her, I wrecked my car. I really could use some prayer."

By staying in communion with the Father, we will see people as He sees them. When we understand what He sees concerning their value, we will be able to love them without getting offended. If we will resist taking the bait of offense, we can seize the opportunity to be a blessing. We were created by God to bless and be a blessing. Inside of us, is the ability to release the power of God that will shift the atmosphere and change a culture. Just a word spoken in love or a kind gesture can change the course of someone's day. Had I clammed up and pouted because she was rude, or had I responded in the same spirit, I could have added just one more thing to what she was going through. The devil would have liked that! He could have snagged two for one.

1 Peter 3:9 "not returning evil for evil or insult for insult, but giving a blessing instead; for you were called for the very purpose that you might inherit a blessing."

If I do not give a blessing, but instead I return evil for evil, I cannot expect a blessing but I can expect the opposite. A curse.

God created everyone with value and the potential to change the world.

God created every person with a created value. Each of us possess the gifts and potential to change the world. The devil, being afraid of our potential and destiny began to destroy us at young age.

When we do not see the value in people, we will not put them first. We will put ourselves first. However, if we will look at people the way that God sees them, as though they are the greatest treasure, we will feel the Father's heart beat. The Father's heart beats with overwhelming love, generosity, compassion and mercy.

Philippians 2:3 "Do nothing from selfishness or empty conceit, but with humility of mind let each of you regard one another as more important than himself;..." We have read it and we have memorized it. But, do we practice it? Is it a revelation to our soul?

A couple of years ago we purchased a new black Expedition. It was perfect and it was gorgeous, sleek shiny black. One day my husband needed something from the grocery store, so we stopped. As I sat in the car, a lady pulled up to my right in her Cadillac. I noticed how lovely she was and beautifully dressed. She appeared to be affluent. As she got out, she slung her door into the side of my new car and went inside. Stunned, I said "Wow, Lord!" I got out to look, and there was my first mark. I got back inside and sat praying, when I saw she returned with one item. As she opened her car door, wham! Again! I thought, "Are you kidding me! No way! Not once, but twice!" As I sat stunned, I looked over at her. Suddenly my eyes were opened and I saw her not as a 'door whacker', but as someone God loved very much. He created her with great destiny and purpose. There was a reason she could whack someone's car door so hard with them sitting there, and not be convicted. Perhaps her heart was breaking, or she was overcome with anger at someone else, or her thoughts were wrapped up somewhere far away from my new car. Or maybe, she was hard of hearing, and did not realize what had happened. If the reason was that she "simply did not care", there is a rooted cause for that as well.

It is the mandate of the Body of Christ to be the force which draws out the greatness in people. The reason we don't see the greatness in people is because we are so focused on ourselves. When we are faced head on with confrontation or offense, we are at a fork in the road. We have the option to be offended or the option to forgive. God will not remove the fork from the middle of the road. However, He will allow you to make the choice to be offended or to choose Love instead! You **will** reap what you sow. "Your choice today will be your harvest tomorrow." That is why God said, "choose life!" I have heard some say, "I will voice my resentment now, and repent later." Really! What are we thinking? Do we not realize that this is not the way of the Kingdom of God?

Joshua 24:15. "If it is disagreeable in your sight to serve the LORD, choose for yourselves today whom you will serve: whether the gods which your fathers served which were beyond the River, or the gods of the Amorites in whose land you are living; but as for me and my house, we will serve the LORD."

My beautiful black Expedition? It's had several good licks since and it's still running well. It's just a car.

When we have been mistreated we immediately **meditate** on the injustice. It is at that point the spirit of offense starts to settle in. Then it begins to build up pressure on our inside until it brings us to the place we have to vent and tell someone. This someone is never **just** someone. The enemy will entice us to tell someone who will sympathize and defend us and take up an offense for us. When we are offended we will look for those people who will agree with us. The spirit of offense is never satisfied with only one person knowing. It has an insatiable appetite and will seek to involve others. I call it, "dumping your nasty into someone else's bucket." In reality, it is planting your seed into their heart.

Seed will produce after its own kind.

Seed will produce after its own kind. **Self pity** has now entered in and is looking for someone to come into agreement and take up an offense. Such is the old saying, "misery loves company." If Susan has offended me, I will seek to justify my anger and hurt. I will race to tell someone my side of the story. And if someone is willing to have an open ear, I will give justification of my wound. Because, it's all about **me**.

The train to disaster has begun to roll and now **gossip** and **slander** join company with the offense team. Gossip and slander are a team whose strategy is contention, division and murder. They work to defame and destroy character. They are known character assassins and should not be found in the Body of Christ.

1 John 3:15 "Everyone who hates his brother is a murderer, and you know that no murderer has eternal life abiding in him."

Proverbs 6:16-19 "There are six things the Lord hates, yes, seven which are an abomination to Him: haughty eyes, a lying tongue, and hands that shed innocent blood, a heart that devises wicked plans, feet that run rapidly to evil, a false witness who utters lies, and one who spreads strife among brothers."

All of these seven things are directly related to **offense**. God, Himself, said He hates them. It would be easy to say then, God hates the spirit of offense because of the destruction and devastation it causes. Offense leaves behind wounded hearts and broken lives.

An offended person affects everyone around him. The spirit of offense creates a chain of events linking offense to offense, affecting many people and then many households. Offense divides family and friends, co-workers, classmates, and neighbors. People have been known to carry an offense for 40 years and even to their graves. The names Hatfield and McCoy bring to mind snickers and subjects of jokes, assuming the two families were crude and backwoods hillbillies. When in fact, they were not. They were esteemed businessmen owning lumber companies who brought income to the whole community and communities around them. Also, they were connected with statesmen and some were war heroes. Their many year disaster began with an assumption that was later found to be false, but it was too late. Actions of retaliation and revenge had already started. Once offended, they carried their retaliation and revenge for many years, resulting in many going to prison and some were hanged by the decision of the courts. The spirit of offense produced devastation and destruction through the families and the community. Parents lost children, children lost parents and siblings, and friends and families were divided. Friendships and marriages were destroyed, never to recover. Their actions produced a legacy of failure, shame, and the subject of jokes and ridicule for generations. The curse came upon the two households could only be stopped by the love of God.

We judge the innocent through the offense that we suffered.

Those who have been hurt and disappointed will judge the innocent through the same spirit of offense that they are driven by. Their form of retaliation is to build a wall around themselves that will protect them from being hurt again. Because they have been hurt so many times in the past, their mindset is one of separation and suspicion. Now they are guarded and live in suspicion, they will **never** be able to love as Christ loves. The wall that they have built becomes a dam that holds back the river called the Love of the Father. The true love of God never focuses on self, but rather, true love only sees through the heart of the Father.

Psalms 101:5. "Whoever secretly slanders his neighbor, him I will destroy; no one who has a haughty look and an arrogant heart, will I endure." We, as children of God cannot afford to fall into the trap of the spirit of offense nor take up an offense for someone else. God hates the fruit of offense. God said He would not tolerate it, so we can be assured that He is going to deal with it, Himself. We can be assured that there will a consequence for our actions.

CHAPTER 7

Why Would I Say That?

After you meditate with resentment, the spirit of offense brings a **judgmental condemning** spirit. We may not carry out the act of manifesting resentment, retaliation, and revenge, but we will judge and condemn others. Judging, condemning and slandering one another, **is** a form of revenge.

I have heard Christians call the offender terrible names and slander them to other people, all as a means to promote sympathy for an offended brother or sister. This can be a conscious or unconscious action. Names like "bum, jerk, a piece of work, white trash" are spoken. If any of these terms have ever come out of your mouth, repent and ask God to show you why you would allow that to manifest. Your spirit man has been defiled by judging and criticism. Those phrases are evidence that a judgmental spirit has taken residence in your spirit man!

In the book of Matthew 15, Jesus was teaching that the way the Pharisees were worshipping was not out of love but rather works. They were religious but not righteous. He proceeded to talk about that which is inside of man, is evidenced by what comes out of the mouth.

Matthew 15:10-20 "And after He called the multitude to Him, He said to them, "Hear and listen. Not what enters into the mouth defiles the man, but what proceeds out of the mouth, this defiles the man. Then the disciples came and said to Him, "Do You know that the Pharisees were offended when they heard this statement?" But He answered and said, "Every plant which My heavenly Father did not plant shall be uprooted. Let them alone; they are blind guides of the blind. And if a blind man guides a blind man, both will fall into a pit." Peter answered and said to Him, "Explain the parable to us." And He said, "Are you still lacking in understanding also? "Do you not understand that everything that goes into the mouth passes into the stomach, and is eliminated? But the things that proceed out of the mouth come from the heart, and those defile the man. "For out of the heart come evil thoughts, murders, adulteries, fornications, thefts, false witness, slanders. These are the things which defile the man; but to eat with unwashed hands does not defile the man."

If you have spoken evil words by calling someone "a jerk, bum or white trash", then you can know that you have received offense into your heart. You judged that person as unworthy. Or, you possibly have associated that person with someone who has caused someone else pain. It was made evident by what came out of your mouth. This is a good thing because you now have opportunity to repent before God and get the cancerous thing out of your spirit. The heart has been exposed. Judging and criticism have gained an advantage through offense.

Matt 12:33-37 "Either make the tree good and its fruit good, or make the tree bad and its fruit bad; for the tree is known by its fruit. You brood of vipers, how can you, being evil, speak what is good? For the mouth speaks out of that which fills the heart. The good man out of his good treasure brings forth what is good; and the evil man brings out of his evil treasure what is evil. And I say to you, that every careless word that men shall speak, they shall render account for it in the day of judgment. For by your words you shall be justified, and by your words you shall be condemned." The word 'careless' means unproductive, unfruitful, and not good for anything useful.

Matthew 7:17-20 "Even so, every good tree bears good fruit, but the bad tree bears bad fruit. A good tree cannot produce bad fruit, nor can a bad tree produce good fruit. Every tree that does not bear good fruit is cut down and thrown into the fire. So then, you will know them by their fruits."

Jesus is making a comparison between fruit trees and what you can discern the tree producing. We, as the Body of Christ, have judged the fruit and condemned the tree. It is not our assignment to condemn the tree. Jesus did say, the final end of that tree will be destruction if it continues to bear bad fruit. Labeling the tree as sorry, good for nothing and not worth their salt, will not help the tree to be restored. The fruit shows the condition of the heart. If it is inevitable we will encounter offenses, then we need to be hearing from our Father at all times!

If the fruit is rotten or unfit to eat, then you can determine that the tree is sickly. Jesus did not say to condemn the tree. But, He was saying when you see the rotted fruit, you will know and understand the expected end for the tree is destruction. So, do something! Where is our compassion and mercy for the tree?

Luke 13:6-9 "and He began telling this parable: "A certain man had a fig tree which had been planted in his vineyard, and he came looking for fruit on it and did not find any. Then he said to the vineyard-keeper, 'Behold, for three years I have come looking for fruit on this fig tree without finding any. Cut it down! Why does it even use up the ground?' And he answered and said to him, 'Let it alone, sir, for this year too, until I dig around it and put in fertilizer; and if it bears fruit next year, fine but if not, cut it down'." Glory be to God, that He clarified that we are not to throw the tree to the burn pile, or there would not be many of us left on the earth!

We fail to recognize the enemy when we judge the person.

We have a responsibility as the Body of Christ, to pray for one another. This is so important for the offender, and for the offended. Yet, we do not pray, because we are looking at the person and we do not recognize the true enemy.

James 5:16 "Therefore, confess your sins to one another, and pray for one another so that you may be healed. The effective prayer of a righteous man can accomplish much." If you are judging and being critical, then you, yourself are a sick tree. People think that this verse applies only to a physical illness. However, many in the Body of Christ are also sick emotionally, financially and spiritually. They are manifesting gossip, slander, taking offense and not forgiving.

Proverbs 18:19 "A brother offended is harder to be won than a strong city, and contentions are like bars of a castle." Another translation referred to it as a gate. A gate does not let people in. The gate is used as separation for protection. It's important that we speak truth to one another, in love, and encourage one another. If we are speaking anything except Truth to them, we are speaking a lie.

Ephesians 4:25. "Therefore, laying aside falsehood, SPEAK TRUTH, EACH ONE OF YOU, WITH HIS NEIGHBOR, for we are members of one another."

Ephesians 4:15-16 "...but, speaking the truth in love, we are to grow up in all aspects into Him, to become in every respect the mature body of him who is the head, even Christ, from whom the whole body being being fitted and held together, by that which every joint supplies, according to the proper working of each individual part, causes the growth of the body for the building up of itself in love."

Ephesians 5:-1-2 "Therefore be imitators of God, as beloved children; and walk in love, just as Christ has loved you and gave Himself up for us, an offering and a sacrifice to God as a fragrant aroma." If we truly see others as more important than ourself, we will be praying for restoration instead of thinking retaliation.

CHAPTER 8

Your Reward Will be the Favor of God.

Genesis 37 presents a beautiful story describing the results when we choose to love, rather than be offended. It describes a 17 year old boy, named Joseph. We can imagine, that just as 17 year old boys today, Joseph didn't always think before he spoke. His chores were to watch his father's sheep along side his stepbrothers. It must have been common for his father, Israel, to send young Joseph to bring back word about the welfare of the brothers and the welfare of the livestock. One day, Joseph brought back a bad report about his brothers to his father, and it was offensive to the brothers. They burned with hate and anger and it added fuel to an already burning fire in their hearts. Israel loved Joseph more than his other sons because he was the son of his old age and so they hated him, and could not speak to him on friendly terms. One day, Joseph had a dream. He told the dream to his brothers, so that they hated him even more. Joseph doesn't appear to be overbearing, devious or arrogant. Although being young and immature, he did not think of his brothers and how the things he said would affect them. Then, he had another dream, and shared it with his brothers as well. It made his brothers more angry. The spirit of offense was working without restraint.

During our walk with the Lord, God will often reveal things to us that are meant for meditation, praise, and focus (I learned this from Pastor Kerry Kirkwood). Not everyone will enter into our happiness. This will cause others to be offended, angry, indignant and jealous. Offended, they will speak words against your prophetic word, your dreams and your visions.

Guard your prophetic words, dreams and visions.

The goal of the enemy is to steal your hope and destiny. If opposition is against you, it's because the enemy is trying hard to get you to cross that line of love, at the cost of your joy, your hope and your destiny.

Joseph's stepbrothers were offended. Realizing what goes into the heart comes out the mouth, you can imagine the verbal abuse that Joseph received. However, Joseph had a relationship with God and trusted God would bring about the things that he dreamed.

We can see the evidence because of the favor that was on his life. Joseph did not let their words separate him from his revelation of God's plans. He had a revelation of who he was, and who his God was to him.

Joseph was spared of murder, thanks to his brother, Reuben. Reuben had the fear of God and suggested that they throw Joseph into a pit. It was Reuben's intentions to retrieve him later and return him safely to his father. The brothers agreed and took Joseph's coat from him and threw him into the pit with no water. A caravan of Ishmaelites passed by and the brothers decide to sell Joseph instead of killing him. In all that Joseph had gone through, I believe he was continually trusting in God. Before his trial ever began, Joseph received two dreams from God which kept him encouraged and at peace. Joseph did not revile or retaliate, but I believe he maintained his relationship with the One who was able to bring his dreams into reality.

If we are going to see the favor of God upon our lives, it is imperative that we know Him intimately.

Genesis 39:1-5 "Now Joseph had been taken down to Egypt; and Potiphar, an Egyptian officer of Pharaoh, the captain of the bodyguard, bought him from the Ishmaelites, who had taken him down there. The LORD was with Joseph, so he became a successful man. And he was in the house of his master, the Egyptian. Now his master saw that the LORD was with him and how the LORD caused all that he did to prosper in his hand. So Joseph found favor in his sight and became his personal servant; and he made him overseer over his house, and all that he owned he put in his charge. It came about that from the time he made him overseer in his house and over all that he owned, the LORD blessed the Egyptian's house on account of Joseph; thus the LORD'S blessing was upon all that he owned, in the house and in the field."

Joseph not only had the favor of God on him, but the favor became a blessing to others. The favor of God is not meant to bless you alone. It is meant to bless those around you so they might see how **Great is your God.** God's favor will draw them into the kingdom. If Joseph had let the spirit of offense rule over him, the favor of God on his life would not have been able to manifest in the way that it. Joseph became **the man** in a world where he was a stranger. He was a Hebrew slave that **glowed in the dark**!

Potiphar's wife tried hard to seduce him, yet he kept integrity. He responded, "Behold, with me here, my master does not concern himself with anything in the house, and he has put all that he owns in my charge. There is no one greater in this house than I, and he has withheld nothing from me except you, because you are his wife. How then could I do this great evil and sin against God?" Joseph's relationship with God preserved him and he saw it not as an offense toward Potiphar, but toward his God.

Offense will hinder the blessing and favor of God.

Joseph was thrown into prison because of her false accusations. "So Joseph's master took him and put him into the jail, the place where the king's prisoners were confined; and he was there in the jail. But the LORD was with Joseph and extended kindness to him, and gave him favor in the sight of the chief jailer. The chief jailer committed to Joseph's charge all the prisoners who were in the jail; so that whatever was done there, he was responsible for it. The chief jailer did not supervise anything under Joseph's charge because the LORD was with him; and whatever he did, the LORD made to prosper." Again, we find the favor of God operating in Joseph's life. Instead of offense, anger and self pity, we find Joseph rising to the top again. It would have been so easy to look at the circumstances around him and blame his brothers for his problems. After all, "he wouldn't have been in this nasty, stinking, urine filled, rat infested dark place if it hadn't have been for them!" However, Joseph kept his course, and stayed in close relationship with his God. This is evidenced when Joseph heard God clearly and was able to interpret the dreams of the baker and the cupbearer. Although not immediately, it ultimately led to his release. The cupbearer forgot to bring Joseph's name up to Pharaoh and so Joseph remained in prison. Then, one day Pharaoh had a dream and the cupbearer remembered Joseph. Joseph was sent to Pharaoh, and God gave Joseph the interpretation of the dream.

Genesis 41:39-44 "So Pharaoh said to Joseph, "Since God has informed you of all this, there is no one so discerning and wise as you are. You shall be over my house, and according to your command all my people shall do homage; only in the throne I will be greater than you." Pharaoh said to Joseph, "See, I have set you over all the land of Egypt." Then Pharaoh took off his signet ring from his hand, and put it on Joseph's hand and clothed him in garments of fine linen and put the gold necklace around his neck. He had him ride in his second chariot; and they proclaimed before him, "Bow the knee!" And he set him over all the land of Egypt. Moreover, Pharaoh said to Joseph, "Though I am Pharaoh, yet without your permission no one shall raise his hand or foot in all the land of Egypt."

The story of Joseph's life is bathed in the favor of God. Joseph had ample opportunities to revile, retaliate and give place to bitterness. However, his right relationship with God preserved him and advanced him into places of authority. His influence created a culture of blessing throughout the land. It spilled over into the lives of others and they entered into his sphere of favor. His faithfulness caused everyone in his sphere of influence to prosper. It could have ended tragically, wiping out a destiny of greatness and the salvation of many people; had Joseph reviled and retaliated in the spirit of offense. Just as it was for Joseph, the reward for resisting and overcoming the spirit of offense, is favor and promotion! In the end, God not only saved the people from famine, but also restored relationships between Joseph and the brothers who wanted to murder him. His brothers lived to witness the favor of God on Joseph and the fulfillment of the two dreams he had. Because Joseph refused to be offended and live in bitterness, his brothers experienced a testimony of love and forgiveness.

CHAPTER 9

There is Power In My Tongue.

The Holy Spirit reveals to us the sin of the tongue has far reaching effects. It has the power to make or break a person's spirit, to bring joy or sorrow, and to lift a person or cast them down. A tale bearer will wreck lives and destroy the happiness of others by gossip and slander.

James 3:2-8 "The tongue a restless evil." The tongue is called the very world of iniquity.

"Who among you is wise and understanding? Let him show by his good behavior, his deeds in the gentleness of wisdom. But if you have bitter jealousy and selfish ambition, do not be arrogant and so lie against the truth. This wisdom is not that which comes down from above, it is earthly, natural, and demonic. For where jealousy and selfish ambition exist, there is disorder and every evil thing. But the wisdom from above is first pure, then peaceable, gentle, reasonable, full of mercy, and good fruits, unwavering without hypocrisy. And the seed whose fruit is righteousness is sown in peace by those who make peace."

Death and life are in the power of the tongue.

Ephesians 4:29 "Let no unwholesome word proceed from your mouth, but only such a word as is good for edification according to the need of the moment, so that it will give grace to those who hear."

Colossians 4:6 "Let your speech always be with grace, seasoned, as it were, with salt, so that you may know how you should respond to each person."

Proverbs 11:9 "With the mouth, the godless man destroys his neighbor."

Proverbs 18:21 "Death and life are in the power of the tongue."

Proverbs 15:4 "a soothing tongue is a tree of life..., but an undisciplined tongue breaks a heart."

Proverbs 11:13 "He who goes about as a tale bearer reveals secrets, but he who is trustworthy conceals a matter."

Proverbs 18:8 "The words of a whisperer are like dainty morsels, and they go down into the innermost parts of the body."

Proverbs 26:20. "For lack of wood the fire goes out, and where there is no whisperer, contention quiets down."

God have not have put it any plainer. The enemy has many more ways to trap us. Offenses are not limited to words. The enemy will manifest himself through the person in body language; such as the rolling of the eyes, the lifting of the chin, snubbing the nose, and the infamous hand signs. Many years before I became a Christian, my husband and I met my mom and others at an auction. My sister-in-law arrived unexpectedly. When I came in with my husband to take our seats, I noticed my sister-in-law sitting behind us. To let her know I was not happy she was there, I gave her a horrible look. No one saw it. Only she and I knew about it. It was a devastatingly mean look and it shocks me to this day that I could be so mean. I crushed her spirit and I am so sorry. The devil has many ways to destroy a person. She was not a Christian and I am sure it cut a deep wound in her. I thought I was a Christian, until my husband was radically born again, and I realized I had no real relationship with God and was not saved at all. My fruit was the fruit testimony of my heart condition.

The magnitude of the offense will never justify unforgiveness.

Offenses can be much more serious. However, no matter how great the offense is, it does not justify unforgiveness and bitterness. Instances when your child has been abused, your spouse has committed adultery, or there has been a crime of rape or murder are all unimaginable situations. These are indeed horrible acts committed against us. However, unforgiveness, bitterness, and revenge are not justifiable even in the light of these atrocities. It is a great place for the grace of God and the healing blood of Jesus to be ministered. The blood of Jesus is the ointment that removes such painful wounds. Only the grace of God can erase those horrible memories. And He wants to! The blood of Jesus has miracle working power. We have heard about that miracle working power for so long, our senses have dulled to it. Our faith has been stolen from us. How will all of this healing happen? It begins with a simple decision to forgive and follow Jesus. We must be **willing to forgive.** He knows that we are hurting. When we lay our pain at His feet, His power will come in and heal us. It's for **our** good that we forgive the offender. In order for us to get from that place called Brokenness to the open spaces of Freedom, we have to forgive.

Matthew 19:26. "And looking upon them, Jesus said to them, "with men this is impossible, but with God, ALL THINGS ARE POSSIBLE!"

CHAPTER 10

We Can Do This! God is With Us!

I Peter 2:19-23 "For this finds favor, if for the sake of conscience toward God, a man bears up under sorrows when suffering unjustly. For what credit is there, if you sin and are harshly treated, you endure it with patience? But, if when you do what is right and suffer for it you patiently endure it, this finds favor with God. For you have been called for this purpose, since Christ also suffered for you, leaving you an example for you to follow in His steps, WHO COMMITTED NO SIN! NOR WAS ANY DECEIT FOUND IN HIS MOUTH and while being reviled, He did not revile in return; while suffering, He uttered no threats, but kept entrusting Himself to Him who judges righteously."

Jesus left the beauty and splendor of Heaven and came into this world to be born of a virgin. He walked as a man, not as God. We want to excuse **our actions** by saying, "well that was Jesus and He was the Son of God." With no excuses permitted, let us remember He came as man, and suffered as we do. Though harshly treated, He did not get offended because He knew what pleased the Father and He entrusted Himself to Him knowing the Father loved Him, even when the world did not.

John 1:10-11 "He was in the world, and the world was made through Him, and the world did not know Him. He came to His own, and those who were His own did not receive Him." They did not have a revelation of who He was. The Holy Spirit had not yet come to convict and enlighten. However, Jesus left us with a Comforter. We have the Holy Spirit to help us. We are without excuse.

2 Corinthians 12:9. "He said, "...My grace is sufficient for you, for power is perfected in weakness..."

Deuteronomy 30:10-16 "If you obey the LORD your God to keep His commandments and His statutes which are written in this book of the law, if you turn to the LORD your God with all your heart and soul. For this commandment which I command you today is not too difficult for you, nor is it out of reach. It is not in heaven, that you should say, 'Who will go up to heaven for us to get it for us and make us hear it, that we may observe it? Nor is it beyond the sea, that you should say, 'Who will cross the sea for us to get it for us and make us hear it, that we may observe it?' But the word is very near you, in your mouth and in your heart, that you may observe it. See, I have set before you today life and prosperity, and death and adversity; in that I command you today to love the LORD your God, to walk in His ways and to keep His commandments and His statutes and His judgments, that you may live and multiply, and that the LORD your God may bless you in the land where you are entering to possess it."

This instruction to Israel was given before Jesus came and poured out His life, and before the Holy Spirit. If God told them then, "It is not too difficult" for them, why do we think it's too hard for us now?

James 1:26 "If anyone thinks himself religious, and yet does not bridle his tongue, deceives his own heart, this man's religion is worthless."

1 John 2:3-6 "By this we know that we have come to know Him, if we keep His commandments. The one who says, "I have come to know Him, and does not keep His commandments is a liar; and the truth is not in him; but whoever keeps His word, in him, the love of God has truly been perfected. By this, we know that we are in Him: the one who says that he abides in Him, ought himself to walk in the same manner as He walked."

The tactic of the enemy is to zero in on the areas in need of strengthening. When we have confidence in what God thinks about us, we no longer need to seek affirmation or approval from others. Weigh what you hear. Can you imagine God saying condemning things to you? What you may be hearing is the voice of the thief.

Who is it that you are listening to?

1 John 4:1 "Beloved, do not believe every spirit, but test the spirits to see whether they are from God, because many false prophets have gone out into the world." Although this does refer to "what you listen to" prophetically, it is an important step we need to take when being rebuked, attacked and reviled. It will you help you a great deal when you hear hurtful things. **Test the spirit**. Is what you heard from the Holy Spirit, or is it from the enemy? If you cannot imagine the Father saying degrading things to you, disregard it. If is does not line up with the Truth, disregard it. **Measure what you hear by the Word of God.** The Word is your measuring tool. If something is said to you in the spirit of anger, don't receive it as Truth. Remember, there is no condemnation in Christ Jesus. So if what is said to you produces shame, guilt and condemnation, you can know that it is not the Holy Spirit speaking. Do not receive it. Let it go, and choose to love in spite of it.

Romans 12:14 "Bless those who persecute you." That doesn't mean you are to stand up in their face and with strained voice and fists clenched behind you and say, "I bless you in Jesus' name!" No! That will not work! When you have understanding about what God sees in them, you can bless them from the heart! By blessing them from the heart, you are slaying a Goliath, and taking your reward. What does that mean? When you bless those that are persecuting you, you halt the enemy. You are hosting the blessing for yourself, to have it work in your behalf, and you release forgiveness towards that person.

Agape love goes beyond the way that people are acting.

Agape love goes beyond the way people are acting. By forgiving, you are displaying the Agape love of the Father. This is something that world has not seen. The church has failed to demonstrate the love of God and they react to offense in the same way that the world does. No wonder the world does not find what it's looking for within the church walls? The Body of Christ has had the mindset that they **go** to church. No! They **are** the Church. Whether you are at the gas pump, or in line at the grocery store, you are the Church.

Jeremiah 29:11 "For I know the plans that I have for you, declares the Lord, plans for welfare, and not for calamity, plans to give you a future and a hope."

The enemy knows the tender areas of your heart, and the wounds from the past. He put them there for a rainy day. Offenses come through those closest to us, as well as those we cannot easily dismiss in our lives; such as employers, family or neighbors. To stand with teeth clenched, does not "an overcomer make."

Deuteronomy 3:22 "Do not fear them, for the Lord Your God, is the one fighting for you."
We are to remember that God said, "the battle belongs to The Lord!"

Romans 8:37 "But in all these things, we overwhelmingly conqueror through Him who loved us." The first thing to remember in the battle, is Jesus with you. He loves you, and He will not leave you.

Jeremiah 31:3 God says that "...He loved you with an everlasting love."

Deuteronomy 31:6 "Be strong and courageous. Do not be afraid or terrified because of them, for the Lord your God goes with you, He will never leave you nor forsake you."

Deuteronomy 20:4 "For the Lord your God is the one who goes with you, to fight for you against your enemies, to save you." In order for God to fight on your behalf, it's important for you to remember that your desire and your words must align with His will.

Position yourself for God to fight for you.

If you will remember the person who abuses you is **not** your enemy, but rather, they are controlled by the enemy of God, you will position yourself for God to fight for you.

It is equally important to remember when we allow the enemy to control **us**, we become the one who offends. God will defend the one we have hurt, including our children. Children are our gift from God and we are equally responsible in how we respond to them as we would be to anyone else. Our words are important. We have to be so very careful what we speak over our children! What we are doing is inadvertently prophesying their future. If we are speaking negative words to them, then those are the things we are sure to see manifest. God created the first man "out of the dust of the ground." It's so important to remember they are soil, and we plant seeds into their spirits. The enemy is crouching at the door, waiting for us to speak words that he can use to destroy them.

Scripture reads, "I am fearfully and wonderfully made," (Psalms 139:14) and the second part of that verse says, "and my soul knows it very well!" It is imperative we know what God thinks about us. Would God say to us, "You can't do anything right. You will never amount to anything good!" No! He is a good Father. **If attitude reflects leadership**, whose leadership are we reflecting?

After we recognize that **it is a spirit** who says, "you can't do anything right or you will never amount to anything," we must take the Word of God in our mouth. Speaking it out so the enemy and the angels can hear us. The Word of God is our weapon. It is the only thing that will defeat the enemy and renew our mind. God said, "We can do all things through Christ who strengthens us." (Philippians 4:13) So the accusation, "you can't do anything right," is a lie.

We "are more than a conqueror..." (Romans 8:37) God calls us, Beloved, Blessed, Chosen, Redeemed, Healed, Righteous and Overcomer... Don't listen to the voices that say, "You are not good enough." What you hearing is **a spirit** speaking through an individual who does not know who they are, nor do they see the created value in you. Don't be offended because they can't see. Go to your Father and pour out your heart to Him. Ask the Him to open their eyes so that they can see. He understands and will put forgiveness in your heart for them. It is His delight to embrace you with His love and heal your heart. Make a choice to love them and bless them instead! You have now have enlisted His help, and He will fight for you!

CHAPTER 11

Can I Call It Righteous Anger?

Unforgiveness is torment. If we have unforgiveness towards anyone, we have sealed the door to our very own prison cell of torture. Until we forgive, the enemy has **legal access** to us. We give him the right to torment and add to our sorrow.

Psalms 109:17 "He also loved cursing, so it came to him; and he did not delight in blessing, so it was far from him. But he clothed himself with cursing as with his garment, and it entered into his body like water, and like oil into his bones." A person who does not forgive, has no ability to bless. Therefore curses come back to him. There was a saying when we were children, "I am rubber, you are glue, your words bounce off me, and stick to you."

The person who refuses to forgive will also judge, gossip and slander. Being offended, she will be resentful and critical. Her unwillingness to forgive extends into other relationships. If people are nice to the person who has hurt her, it offends her the more, and it causes more division. Neither does she want to see others enjoy fellowship with the one who offended her. She will retaliate by separating herself and destroy the other relationships. When you see this behavior, remember these are **spirits**. If she truly had a revelation of what was going on, she would not behave in such a manner. Meet her with forgiveness and love, in order that she might repent and be restored.

Matthew 6:14 "For if you forgive men for their transgressions, your Heavenly Father will also forgive you."

Ephesians 4:26-27 "Be ANGRY, AND yet DO NOT SIN; do not let the sun go down on your anger, and do not give the devil an opportunity." This is a scripture that has not been taught correctly and allows the Body of Christ to feel justified for their anger.

We are not justified to be angry at the offender.

We are not justified to be angry at the person who offends. Truly, offenses such as adultery, molestation, and murder are much greater than the offense of having your car keyed. However, "My grace is sufficient for you, for power is perfected in weakness." Yes, we will feel anger ministering to us. The spirit of anger is very real but we have a choice to run to the Father immediately! If we will run to our Father quickly, and seek His grace, which He said is sufficient; we **will** find grace "in time of need." In our weakness we will receive His power to overcome the enemy.

The world defines righteous anger as a "justifiable reactive emotion of anger" due to mistreatment, insult or malice. It is also called the "sense of injustice." The term "reactive emotion of anger" indicates an outburst of resentment or reviling due to mistreatment, insult or malice. Scripture speaks of the opposite. Such as, "revile not," or "not returning insult for insult." How can anyone get angry without being offended? By recognizing the source is a spirit. Recognize who the real enemy is! If we will recognize that we are confronted by a spirit, we will **avoid the temptation** to be offended. We will see that we are being set up for disaster.

James 1:20 "for the anger of man does not achieve the righteousness of God." If we give in to the the spirit of anger, we will reproduce of its kind. Just as apple seeds produce apple trees, and cherry seeds reproduce of its kind, sin will reproduce of its kind.

Ephesians 5:6-8 "Let no one deceive you with empty words, for because of these things the wrath of God comes upon the sons of disobedience. Therefore, do not be partakers with them; for you were formerly darkness, but now you are Light in the Lord; walk as children of Light." But we should have also, put aside, anger, wrath, malice, slander, and abusive speech from our mouth, not lying to one another, putting to death the old self with its evil behavior, and having put on the new man who is being renewed to a true awareness of the image of the One who created us. This scripture is very clear that anger produces the wrath of God. He calls **the angry person** a son of disobedience. However, we as lovers of God do not walk there any longer. We used to but our hearts have been renewed to the mind of Christ. According to this verse, we are not to be angry at the offender regardless of how heinous the act. This is difficult to receive unless we **recognize who our true enemy really is**! The enemy tried something that he was pretty sure would work! He is confident after training us to focus on our feelings and our opinions, that we will submit to the spirit of offense. God has a much better way. You have an option to choose love and receive blessings.

Mark 3:5 "And after looking around at them with anger, grieved at their hardness of heart, He said to the man, "Stretch out your hand." And he stretched it out, and his hand was restored." Jesus was not angry at the people, He was angry at the spirit of religion He was seeing. The verse says that He was grieved at their hardness of heart. I believe that He was angry at **the religious spirit** that held them in bondage to the point they could not believe. The church has justified their anger, and responses in anger, as righteous indignation.

James 3:10 “from the same mouth come both blessing and cursing. My brethren, these things ought not to be this way.” In other words, we cannot justify any angry response, such as resentment, reviling and retaliation as righteous anger.

This is not a matter of biting our tongue or merely keeping our mouth shut. There is much effort in doing so, but where is Love? Jesus said, “love your enemies, and pray for those who persecute you.” How do you do that while you are faced with someone who is yelling with red face and wild eyes? The greatest revelation that the church has missed, is being able to see the offender as God sees them.

Look into the soul of the offender through the Father’s eyes.

You must understand the offender and how the enemy is manipulating them. The offender’s primary characteristic is **brokenness**. They have been wounded and they act out of the wounded soul. If you will look behind the face and look into the soul of the offender, you will see the face of the enemy of God. They wouldn’t do what they do, if they really knew what they should know. If they really understood the curses and judgement that they heap upon themselves when they offend, they wouldn’t behave the way that they do. Look behind the face and listen to what is being said. Is the Spirit of God telling you what a failure you are, or is it the enemy of your soul? Is God bringing up your past, or is it the enemy? God said, "He separates our sin as far as east is to west." (Psalms 103:12) If God has remitted our sins, then it cannot be God who is throwing our failures in our face to bring condemnation and shame. If God does not remember our sins, why do we remember and allow the enemy to bring condemnation?

Romans 8:1 "There is now, no condemnation for those who are in Christ Jesus." If you listen to who is really doing the talking and recognize the true torment of the offender, you will look with spiritual eyes and see their pain. When you begin to care more about the offender than the offense. Choose with your heart to love them and God will move in your behalf.

God, Himself, will fight the battle because the battle becomes a battle between the enemy and God. (And He never loses.) "Don't let what they don't know, affect what you do know. Do not allow the sin working in them to produce sin in you." The enemy's strategy is to get us to move out of love because he knows that God cannot work without the presence of love. When we move out of love, we make provision for the enemy to work through offense with the purpose of manifesting hate, anger, and murder. God wants us to see with spiritual eyes so we can see the offender as He sees them. Do you think that God looks down at the offender, and says, "Wow! What a jerk! What a piece of work he is! I wasted My time creating that one!"

NO! Absolutely NOT! What God sees is a broken vessel that needs someone to step up and see their value and love them so they might be healed and restored from what is tormenting them.

People speak out of the wounds of their heart.

Many years ago, I had to serve notice to someone. The woman, who had official military status, was not happy. As I came out of my office door, she cornered me. Screaming and with arms flailing, she came nose to nose with me. As I looked up the bridge of her nose, and witnessed the fire in her eyes, one thought repeated itself over and over. "She is going to hit me." She was younger, taller and more physically fit. Even though she was in the wrong, and displayed behavior unfitting for an officer, I said nothing. My husband was standing to my side, and I have no remembrance of him saying anything, for which I am so grateful. When she had said all that she wanted to say, she turned and left. My thoughts were reeling with, "I thought for sure she was going to hit me!" My husband turned to me and said, "Wow! I thought that she was going to hit you!" Who was ministering with those thoughts? It was the spirit of offense. My point in sharing this story is, I could have reviled with words. I could have retaliated and argued my case. Then, after I recovered from her blow, I could have ruined her career. But thanks be to God, He prevailed. Very shortly after, we were realized to be a trustworthy and safe place for her very small daughter, who became a precious member in our household. When the mother had to go on international assignments, she considered our home to be the safest place for her daughter. The woman was a precious single mom who struggled very hard and had a destiny and purpose. She would have never acted that way if she only thought it through first. The world would say that she lost her head. But in reality, she was offended, fearful, and angry. She **meditated** on resentment and so she reviled. That is what losing your head is. When the enemy overcomes you, you do things out of hate. Praise God that it wasn't any worse than that, and she didn't fall into retaliation and murder.

People speak out of the wounds in their heart. It was easy to see where her offense came in. If we will look and listen to what is being said, we will hear the fear and wounds in the heart of the person doing the screaming.

CHAPTER 12

The Weapon of Comparison and Legal Access.

Luke 6:44 "For each tree is known by its own fruit. For men do not gather figs from thorns, nor do they pick grapes from a briar bush. The good man out of the good treasure of his heart brings forth what is good; and the evil man out of the evil treasure brings forth what is evil; for his mouth speaks from that which fills his heart."

To learn testing through fire, everyone should work the retail market at sometime in their life. You can be sure that the retail market will purify your soul through fire!

One day, someone was having a bad day and became angry with me. They said, "you..............!", and "you............!", and "you........!"

I walked away condemned, disappointed, humiliated and utterly broken in despair. Attempting and determined to bless them, I cried out to the Lord. I said, "Father! I could have handled one thing and maybe two things, but really Lord, three was too much!" It felt as if all the life had been punched out of me. Then God spoke to my heart, and said, "What did you hear?" I answered, "They said,......." and "they said......." and "they said......" Again He said, "what did you hear?" My answer was the same. The third time He asked, "What did you hear?" I responded, "Okay! What did I hear?" In His calm and gentle way, He answered, "You heard their **thoughts**." Only God can say something so profound in four words or less. It was a revelation from Heaven which not only healed my heart, but it set me on a path to change my thinking that day!

Who told me that lie?

This revelation can be as exciting as a yearly bonus if we will take it to heart! Since, out of the mouth, the heart speaks, we would do well to recognize who is behind the words that we hear!

Take care what you hear, measure it and line it up with the Word of God. Ask yourself, "who told me that lie!" Was it the Holy Spirit or the enemy? If it was the enemy, cast it down! Jesus told us that the devil is the father of lies.

I have never fried chicken in my life, but I use this illustration as example. For a moment, let's imagine a young wife in her kitchen attempting this amazing feat. She wants to surprise her husband for his birthday and make the homemade nostalgic meal of fried chicken complete with side dishes. Poring over book after book, and reviewing the ever-informative cooking sites, she finds a recipe that she thinks she can handle. Thanking God for the man who butchered and the man who plucked the chicken so she didn't have to, she begins her preparations. It's a struggle because she is not a skilled cook, but she finally nears a completion of what was a monumental task. Standing and checking everything, she is pleased with her accomplishment. The door opens and in walks her husband, who throws his jacket over the chair and says, "What's that awful smell?"

With a proud response, she replies, "Happy Birthday! It's fried chicken!" He says, "It looks like road kill." Ignoring the sting, she can see that it doesn't exactly look like the pictures that she saw in the recipe book photos but is not bad for a first attempt. He returns in his pajama bottoms after washing up. As they sit down, he said, "Did you mean for it to be this brown?" And then, "You should get my mom to teach you how to make fried chicken. No one can beat my mom's fried chicken. I have never seen fried chicken this hard or brown before." Then the the potatoes were too salty and the gravy too thick.

"It's my birthday, and I just thought we could have gone out to get a steak tonight. No one thinks to ask me what I might like to do. No one cares what I think. And no birthday cake!" Suddenly she realizes in the busyness and stress of trying to make the perfect dinner, she forgot to pick up the cake from the bakery! Shame and condemnation are overwhelming her as she feels like a total failure. Lastly he responds with "I think I will just go to bed." He leaves his dinner on the table.

This illustration reeks of disappointment and hurt. We can feel the emotional pain flood over her soul. Some might look at him and say, "Wow! He was thoughtless and was being a real jerk." (Caution: beware of judging.) But let's look at this deeper. He woke with the expectation the world would feel his excitement over his birthday. In the rush to get the kids ready for school, the "todo" was small and barely acknowledged. He leaves for work and remembers he had not completed his assignment, which he needed to have completed it before his boss comes in. He had lingered at the house too long, desiring just a little more attention due his special day. On the way to work he was stopped for speeding in a school zone, all because his thoughts were somewhere else. Although he was blessed with only a warning, he could not **see** the blessing to appreciate it. After all, "his family should care more about his birthday than anyone else." He gets to work to find the boss was there early to receive the much needed presentation. There were no balloons, no cards, no "Happy Birthday, man." The day turned out to be awful, with one bad incident after another. He thinks, "Well, we will just go out and order a steak tonight, and maybe I will treat myself to a dessert!" As he is leaving, someone in the office says, "Oh yeah, I heard it was your birthday. Happy Birthday!" Too late! The day was already a bummer. No one really cares. When he gets home, expecting his wife to say, "Let's go out for a steak for your birthday", he finds really brown fried chicken and it smells. So he puts on his pajamas because he is going to eat, call the day a wash, and go to bed.

Although merely an illustration, it is not actually extreme. It speaks of the trials in the lives of a busy family and the all too familiar "setup" situation of birthday expectations. More importantly though, this illustration shows who is working behind the scenes creating disaster, disappointment and wounds. As far as she is concerned, he may never see fried chicken again, unless his mom makes it. What could possibly make it worse?

The next day, his mother celebrates his birthday with a fried chicken dinner and a birthday cake! He said to his wife, "Don't you just love Mom's fried chicken? You should get her to teach you how to make fried chicken!" She thinks, "Honey, you will rue the day, when you see fried chicken come out of our kitchen again!" (The day before, offense and resentment had already entered into her heart along with retaliation. This statement exposes a form of retaliation. The sting she felt was from the spirit of offense, the bait of the enemy.) Did you notice the **thought** he had, "we will just go out for a steak dinner" came out of his mouth towards her later when he said, "I thought you would say, let's go out for a steak dinner". His thought manifested through his mouth, creating an expectation for her to fulfill. Unfulfilled expectations always give way to the spirit of offense.

The tactics and tools of the enemy are exposed in this scenario. Her expectations that 'he would appreciate a nostalgic dinner' and 'he would be impressed with her effort', were in error. She handled the 'road kill' comment well enough. However, the comparison to his mother hit deep! It was meant to! The devil knows how and when to use that weapon. The weapon of **comparison** is powerful in his arsenal. It is meant for the victim to feel second rate, less than, and inferior to someone else. No one wants to think they are second, especially in marriage. This weapon works every time.

Another weapon in his bag of tricks is failure. When she forgot the cake, it was the tipping point for disaster. When the spirit of offense uses failure, it's desire is to bring in condemnation and shame, leaving the individual with resentment and unforgiveness. We are all responsible for forgiving one another but we must also forgive ourselves. Many autoimmune diseases have been linked to **unforgiveness towards self**. It is vital that we do not lean into failure and hold unforgiveness towards ourselves.

Her husband huffs off to bed taking depression with him and the spirit of offense is left to torment her. It brings the weapon of rejection and separation. This weapon enlarges the place for anger to operate and strengthens the spirit of offense to create greater division. After all her plans and high hopes, she is left to clean up the mess of the day.

His excitement about the day was met with disappointment and his expectations were left unfulfilled. It ended in criticism, complaining, anger, rejection, self pity, and depression. He was **blinded** to her efforts and her hurt. It was all about unfulfilled expectations. He thought no one cared enough. The devil brought thoughts that he was not appreciated. Although he went to bed to forget about it all, the devil begins preparations for the morning when he wakes up. Until there is repentance and forgiveness, the stage is set for another round of offense. The spirit of offense prepares to meet him in the morning to build a greater plan of destruction.

Unfulfilled expectations are the breeding grounds for offense.

Satan knows that he did not de-throne God, but he is pretty sure that he can dethrone Him from our heart. His schemes are often subtle and so he waits, and he builds and waits, and builds and waits, until he has an substantial fortress in which to control from. And we never see it coming! Those little stings, those little digs, those fiery darts are wicked and are set in place to accumulate until we are overwhelmed. That is why it is so very important to guard our hearts and our thoughts. The schemes of the enemy have not changed.

Ephesians 6:10-17. "Finally, be strong in the Lord and in the strength of His might. Put on the whole armor of God, that you may be able to stand firm against the schemes of the devil. For our struggle is not against flesh and blood, but against rulers, against the powers, against the world forces of this darkness, against spiritual forces of wickedness in the heavenly places. Therefore, take up the full armor of God, that you may be able to resist in the evil day, and having done everything, to stand firm." (You cannot withstand something that never comes your way.) "Stand firm therefore, having girded your loins with truth, having put on the breastplate of righteousness, and having shod your feet with the preparation of the gospel of peace; in addition to all, taking up the shield of faith with which you will be able to extinguish all the flaming missiles of the evil one. And take the helmet of salvation, and the sword of the Spirit, which is the word of God."

The problem for the Church is they have not recognized the stings and fiery darts as subtle weapons in the maneuvers of war. Satan is a smooth liar and he will slowly build his fortress. It's those stings, those little foxes, that come into the vineyard to destroy. The fox is opportunistic. He looks for opportunity where there is prey. We have an opportunistic enemy who seeks to destroy. The fox is deceitful, sneaky and he slips around doing his damage. He is quiet, resourceful and does not alert you of his presence. Often he goes unnoticed, until destruction has already begun to manifest.

2 Corinthians 4:18 "while we look not at the things which are seen, but at the things which are not seen;...." This verse, though talking about momentary afflictions, does make a distinction between a seen world and an unseen world. It's in this unseen world that the

enemy is able to work throughout the day. We do not see what people are going through causing them to behave and react the way that they do.

2 Timothy 3:12 "And indeed, all who desire to live godly in Christ Jesus will be persecuted."
If we live a godly life, we will be persecuted. You can be sure of this. Remember, Jesus said, "Offenses will come". It is not a question of '**if** offenses come'. The question is, how will we respond **when** offenses do come.

Matthew 5:10-12 "Blessed are those who have been persecuted for the sake of righteousness, for theirs is the kingdom of heaven. Blessed are you when men cast insults at you, and persecute you, and say all kinds of evil against you falsely on account of Me. Rejoice and be glad, for your reward in heaven is great, for so they persecuted the prophets who were before you." Many will say, "Well, that refers to standing for the Gospel." When you choose to love and be like Christ, "the enemy who seeks to steal, kill and destroy," will be provoking you to get you to lay down righteousness and pick up unrighteousness.

The spirit of offense is seeking legal access.

Romans 8:33-34 "Who will bring a charge against God's elect? God is the one who justifies; who is the one who condemns? Christ Jesus is He who died, yes, rather who was raised, who is at the right hand of God, who also intercedes for us."

The spirit of offense is seeking legal access. If the President of the United States gives you legal access to the White House, you are privileged to go throughout the White House at anytime of day that you wish. No one can override that privilege until the President revokes that privilege. When we fall to the snare of the spirit of offense, we give the enemy legal access, until we repent. However, once we repent we revoke his privileges to legal access.

Job 6:23-24 "Deliver me from the hand of the adversary, redeem me from the hand of the tyrants, teach me, and I will be silent and show me how I have erred."

Ecclesiastes 10:20 "Furthermore, in your bedchamber do not curse a king, and in your sleeping rooms do not curse a rich man, for a bird of the heavens will carry the sound and the winged creature will make the matter known." This proverb is relating how we can curse someone under our breath alone in our room, or even without using their name. The winged creature represented is an angel and will bring the thing you have said, to the light.

Luke 12:2-3 "But there is nothing covered up that will not be revealed, and hidden that will not be known. Accordingly, whatever you have said in the dark will be heard in the light, and what you have whispered in the inner rooms will be proclaimed upon the housetops."

For years, it was a concerted effort for me not to say a negative word about building contractors. In our city we have many good contractors and quite a few unskilled or unconcerned, who are looking only for their check at the end. A perfect job is not their motivating force. I would see things that I felt were outrageously substandard work and yet they expected payment for it from unsuspecting buyers. I finally arrived at the place where I could keep quiet without telling the client a horror story. Then one day I was out of town on a job and the conversation came around to a house that had become a nightmare. It was the common result of the builder not doing his job. I commented about a similar story but mentioned no name. We said our good byes and I got into the car. I didn't get to the end of the driveway when I heard My Father say, "You did it again." I responded, "I didn't say any names!" I heard Him so clearly that I had to stop my car! He said, "You knew who you were slandering, I knew who you were slandering, and the angels knew who you slandered!" Wow, I know what angels do! They carry out the spoken word! I repented quickly! You might say, "Well, I don't think that it's that serious."

Hebrews 1:14 “Are they not all angels ministering spirits sent out to render service for the sake of those who will inherit salvation?”

Psalms 109:17 “He also loved cursing, so it came to him; And he did not delight in blessing, so it was far from him.”

Proverbs 26:2 “Like a sparrow in its flitting, like a swallow in its flying, so a curse without cause does not alight.” A curse cannot light without a cause. That describes “legal access”.

I Peter 3:10-12 “For, let him who means to love life and see good days, refrain his tongue from evil and his lips from speaking guile. And let him turn away from evil and do good; let him seek peace and pursue it. For the eyes of the Lord are upon the righteous and His ears attend to their prayer, but the face of the Lord is against those who do evil.” If we are walking with God with a heart to do His will, repenting when we fall, God calls us righteous. This occurs, not by any works or performance of our own. The blood of Jesus is what He sees when He looks at us and the Holy Spirit creating in us a mature man. We are righteous because of the blood. A heart yielded to Him.

How you respond is crucial to your blessing.

Ecclesiastes 5:6 “Do not let your speech cause you to sin and do not say in the presence of the ‘messenger of God’ that it was a mistake.

Why should God be angry on account of your voice and destroy the work of your hands?" We can see here, that what you say and how you respond is crucial for your blessing.

Job 22:28 "You will also declare a thing, and it will be established for you; so light will shine on your ways." What we speak, we will see. The messengers of God are ministering spirits who will carry out what we say.

Psalms 141:3 "Set a guard, O LORD, over my mouth; Keep watch over the door of my lips." This is to avoid giving the enemy legal access. Satan is not only an opportunist, he is a legalist! He is crouching at our door waiting for us to speak something that he can use to accuse us, or do something that he can use against us for a hostile takeover.

At our shop we minister to people who come to us for prayer. Once they repent of holding unforgiveness towards someone, God heals them physically as well as emotionally nearly every time. The same works for fear. Both fear and unforgiveness keep us in bondage. If we walk in offense the enemy has legal access to invade our bodies with sickness and disease, and to invade our relationships, our finances and our Church body. When a husband, who is the head of the house, walks in fear and unforgiveness the entire household is affected. Likewise, if a pastor, the shepherd of the flock, is wounded by the past wrongs of others and is offended, he unknowingly gives legal access to the enemy to infiltrate his congregation. That's why it is so important for the Church to cover their pastors and leaders with prayer. Let's don't wait to pray when we hear about the strife! We should be praying for our pastors continuously.

Worship leaders are accosted because someone has a complaint about the music. It's too loud, too old, too new. However, the complainant never stops with the worship leader, and the next stop will be to the pastor. Shepherds have had to become more like the elementary school teacher who has been assigned to playground watch. This should not be this way. Pastors are called to minister what they hear from the Lord and demonstrate what the love of the Father looks like. They are not called to be babysitters and squabble referees. It's time for the Body to become mature sons and daughters.

The very word "unforgiveness" sparks denial.

Pastors get abused and used, and their wives are often mistreated. Their children should not have to be subjected to seeing their parents mistreated. If pastors are not watchful, they will unknowingly hold unforgiveness for those past wounds. The spirit of offense, operating through wound after wound, has been given legal right over him and everything he is called to do. The pastor may be a good shepherd and care deeply about the flock, but the spirit of offense and the wounds of the past will always keep him guarded. He can never give himself to **all** of the flock. Those who remind him of someone who offended him, will not get past the now guarded door of his heart. This is an unconscious response to fear, suspicion and hurt that will keep him distrustful. It is a self preservation reaction, because he doesn't want to be hurt again. And who can blame him? Religious people are meaner than junk yard dogs. The shepherd can still operate in the gifts that God has given him because the gifts of God are irrevocable. Though he might walk in divine healing and have revelatory wisdom or walk in the gift of the prophetic, he can still give the enemy legal access through unforgiveness.

The very word unforgiveness sparks denial in us. However, if we are reminded of what others have done to us, we will be **guarded** because of it. We must acknowledge that we still have not completely forgiven as Christ forgives. Christ does not remember what we have done in the past. There is no accounting of it. Love does not take into account a wrong suffered.

We will never overcome what we refuse to acknowledge.

We will never overcome that which we refuse to acknowledge. The word forgive is defined as, "to give up all account of; to remit." In other words, as if it has never happened. Forgiveness does not leave us guarded. We can never truly love others as Christ loved us, when we are guarded. Because others have hurt you, it doesn't mean that everyone else is like that. The way that the Body of Christ has abused one another, especially our pastors, is horrible and we suffer the consequences for it. However, the pastor is no different from the flock in regards to unforgiveness. If the shepherd cannot forgive, he has given the enemy legal access to silently slither through the congregation. The enemy will continue to build on the lack of forgiveness to secure and retain his legal right. He will bring more opportunities of disappointment and offense to wound the shepherd further. This secures the enemy's position by keeping things stirred up. The Body cannot prosper until all offenses are forgiven and healing comes and only then will legal access be denied. We are all of one body, one church. The church is not a building or a particular assembly. That is old wine skin thinking. We **are** the Body of Christ, and we have a responsibility to be praying for the shepherds of every church, not just the one that we are attending. People have no idea of what pastors endure. Their phone never stops ringing, their lives are not private, the complaints and suggestions never end, and the enemy never takes a break. Those who choose to live godly will be persecuted. It would do us well, to imagine what they go through. Let us be very wary that we never judge them... for anything! If we judge them, we give legal access to the enemy in our own lives. If we talk about them, we have judged them already. Neither should pastors judge people based on personal wounds they have sustained themselves.

Psalms 62:3 "... How long will you assail a man, that you may murder him, all of you, like a leaning wall, like a tottering fence? They have counseled only to thrust him down from his high position; they delight in falsehood; they bless with their mouth, but inwardly they curse."

Be slow to speak and quick to listen, because the secret is Love.

Psalms 39:1 "I said, I will guard my ways that I may not sin with my tongue; I will guard my mouth as with a muzzle." If we will guard our tongues and our hearts, we will be able to stand against the wiles of the devil. The secret is Love. Love has a name, and He is amazing. If we will be slow to anger, slow to speak and will listen, we will be able to pick up the heart beat of The Father. If we will **see** the person as an incomplete work and that God isn't finished with them yet, we will never put our mouth on them or judge them. As we also, are an unfinished work, would we not want the same grace and mercy for ourselves?

1 Peter 1:6 "In this you greatly rejoice, even though now for a little while, if necessary, you have been distressed by various trials, that the proof of your faith, being more precious than gold which is perishable, even though tested by fire..." When someone has

misunderstood our intentions or something that we have said, we can know that a devil is there perverting and creating opportunity for offense.

1 Peter 1:13-14 “Therefore, gird your minds for action, keep sober in spirit, fix your hope completely on the grace to be brought to you at the revelation of Jesus Christ. As obedient children, do not be conformed to the former lusts which were yours in your ignorance,…” To overcome the spirit of offense, we will have to keep sober in spirit, prepare our minds for action, and be ready to return their hate with Love. We cannot revert to the former lusts that tempt us. Former lusts entreated us to revile with insult for insult. Our belief system was immature. So, our actions were earthly, natural and demonic. When we have stumbled and fallen to the spirit of offense, it is because we were not expecting it. It catches us by surprise. That is the reason that Peter said, “be sober in spirit”.

2 Corinthians 2:10 “But one whom you forgive anything, I forgive also; for indeed what I have forgiven, if I have forgiven anything, I did it for your sakes in the presence of Christ, in order that no advantage would be taken of us by Satan, for we are not ignorant of his schemes.” Satan seeks an advantage, and that advantage for

him, comes with our negative responses when we are offended. Isn't it time for us to be more aware of his schemes?

Truly, time is fleeting and we shall all be accountable for how we finish. Will we be able to look into His eyes when He asks, "Did you learn how to love?"

Chapter 13

Look Behind the Pretty Face.

Things are not always as they appear. We need to look behind the face of the offender and when we do, we will see the offended. The names are changed in these three very different friends. Michael is married to Betty. He is a quiet, non contentious man. One day Michael informed Betty that his sister, Gloria and her husband were coming for the weekend. Dread immediately washed over Betty at the thought of seeing them again, much less, having to entertain them for a weekend! Many years ago Gloria made a comment to Betty about her dress, saying, "How quaint. Is it homemade? I bet you made it yourself." Gloria could afford the best and dressed as such. Although it had been said many years ago, it stung as if it were yesterday. Betty could hardly sleep as her mind ran away with the thoughts of the past. The next morning she relived the moment again and again. Memories of how Michael stood and said nothing as his sister humiliated her. It rekindled thoughts of resentment towards her husband that she thought were gone. She meditated on it while she showered and then later, while she made breakfast for Michael. When he asked her for something, she snapped at him abruptly. The more she meditated on what Gloria had done, the more she burned. She felt all those degrading feelings of embarrassment again. She thought to herself, "If she says one thing to me, or even looks at me wrong, I am going to tell her what I **think**! I will see how she likes it!" That night Gloria and her husband arrived in time for dinner. Betty thought, "Of course and without so much as a notice!" Thoughts of retaliation swam through her head. Michael answered the door and he immediately noticed that Gloria's countenance had changed. There was something very different about her. However, Betty could not see anything good about Gloria because she was seeing through the eyes of bitterness. What Betty did not know was that Gloria had given her life to Jesus and came to share her experience with her family.

Betty's wounds are easy to see. In fact, she is all too familiar to many of us. A closer look at Betty's heart helps us to understand how the enemy works. Betty was the child of a single parent who struggled to make ends meet. She did not have the luxuries that Gloria had while growing up and there was a wound in her heart because of it. She knew Gloria did not know what it was like to struggle and be embarrassed of homemade clothes. The scheme of the enemy was to shoot a fiery dart at the very wound he had prepared many years ago. He silently worked for years, strategically planning on her destruction. She had a low self esteem and felt rejected by many. Betty felt like she didn't fit in. Not having a father at home, she never felt protected. Unknowingly Betty wanted someone to be her protector and take the place of the father that she never knew. Michael disappointed her when he didn't protect her from the words of his sister. No one understood her pain of being fatherless. But Holy Spirit knows!

Michael is a neat, small built man who knew what it was like to be bullied. Therefore, he hated confrontation. Although he and Gloria grew up somewhat privileged, Michael never felt that he fit in anywhere. He preferred things to go along smoothly without incident. His father was not physically abusive, however Michael always felt the pain from **impossible expectations.** Suffering from low self esteem, he saw himself as an outcast. Michael was bullied at school for his size and his father's occupation. He kept his anger on the inside and suffered physically. He couldn't be the protector that Betty always wanted. Fear ruled over him.

Michael's sister, Gloria is beautiful. Michael and Gloria were preacher's kids. They suffered greatly for it. Every Sunday they went home to Sunday dinner and roasted the congregation. Dinner consisted of helpings of slander, side dishes of gossip and resentment, criticism, and judgement. Deep inside of Gloria was the awareness that if they were talking about people, then surely people were talking about them. Her mother put a large emphasis on how perfect they had to be in their attire. Gloria knew though they looked good on the outside, they did not live in Godly behavior. It was constant fear that someone would find out everything that they portrayed was merely superficial. She lived on edge. Gloria feared exposure. She knew she could not live up to her parents' expectations any more than those in the church could. She carried wounds of shame, low self esteem, rejection, self preservation, and criticism coupled with slander and gossip. To escape the pain she retreated further into vanity. Being trained to perform, she was an over achiever and understood how to perform well. She never saw the real Jesus! Sadly, neither did her parents. Looking deeper, we see that though they were in ministry, they lost sight of Jesus and their purpose. The invited guests at the dinner table were **judging, criticism** and **gossip**. The presence of these spiritual guests is an indicator that the shepherd of the congregation and the shepherd of the family had been wounded. There is a myriad of methods the enemy uses to derail a shepherd. One is complaining within the church body. Another is unfulfilled expectations. Somewhere he suffered many wounds that allowed the root of bitterness to manifest at the table. It is very sad. A calling of God had been damaged and left a generation groomed to carry a legacy of unforgiveness. The church body was spiritually and physically sick because the head was sick. The testimony to those around them displayed something that did not look like anything the world would want.

The wisdom of God is to know how to use the knowledge of God correctly.

It is our mantle as sons and daughters of God to recognize the work of the enemy and pray for one another. James 5:16 "Therefore, confess your sins to one another, and pray for one another so that you may be healed. The effective prayer of a righteous man can accomplish much."

Colossians 1:9-12 "For this reason also, since the day we heard of it, we have not ceased to pray for you and to ask that you may be filled with the knowledge of His will in all spiritual wisdom and understanding, so that you will walk in a manner worthy of the Lord, to please Him in all respects, bearing fruit in every good work and increasing in the knowledge of God; strengthened with all power, according to His glorious might, for the attaining of all steadfastness and patience; joyously giving thanks to the Father, who has qualified us to share in the inheritance of the saints in Light."

If we are not walking in a manner worthy of the Lord, then we lack spiritual wisdom and understanding. We do not have a revelation of the knowledge of His will for us. The wisdom of God is to know how to use the knowledge of God correctly. A tree bearing bad fruit is a tree in need of healing. It needs attention. We pray for one another so the Father can till up the ground around the root of the tree, feed, fertilize and water. What we need is wisdom and love. As the Church, we are to be ever increasing in the knowledge of God. Knowing Him in ever increasing ways and learning His character. In every aspect, we are growing in the understanding that He is all that He says He is. His name is Trustworthy, Faithful, and True. He is patient and long suffering. Merciful and compassionate are His ways. Our desire is to know Him in a deeper way. It is in communion with Him, that we get to know Him better, and walk in a manner that is worthy.

When I was eleven or twelve years old, I loved to be in church. It must have been about a mile walk to the church. It could have been a shorter distance if I were to cut through the cemetery. However, there was a caretaker who lived there. Everyone said he was crazy and we were warned not to cut through there. (Another wounded man.) People who lived in the homes overlooking the cemetery, would gossip and slander him. Back then, we had unmotorized push mowers. Imagine taking care a large cemetery with those to work with! I used to wonder about him as I walked around the three sides of the cemetery. Even as small child, I had a desire to talk to him and know more about him. He was so alone.

It was a cold night in Baltimore and there had been a heavy snow, but I wanted to go to church. My mom gave me permission to go. I wore pants in order to help keep warm. Even today, I remember the walk was difficult because there was so much snow that week. The snow was going into my boots. When I got to the church, having stomped the snow off my boots I took my place on the right side, second row. For me, there was no better place to be.

The pastor came over to me and instead of greeting me, he said that I needed to call my parents and have someone pick me up to take me home. He said, "Pants are not allowed in the church." (We all gasp at that mindset today.) Being raised up on rules and wanting to please God in any way the pastor said would be pleasing, I wasn't the least bit offended. However, my mom was not happy! That offended her. As a parent we understand that. In defense of the pastor, he had **twisted thinking**. Somewhere he had been taught that reverence to God was demonstrated by what you wore inside the building. Because his belief system had perimeters regarding dress, there was no grace afforded to a little girl who walked through about a foot of snow to get to church. Neither was there grace from the mother for his twisted thinking. The pastor was offended, the mother was offended and the little girl was cold and didn't want to miss anything going on at the church!

Before you get offended, listen to the Holy Spirit.

People leave the church body in a huff for much less than that. Things like the color of the carpet, the music, someone moved the seating arrangement, the amount of money spent on flowers. We have so missed God. Before you get offended by what someone says, listen to the Holy Spirit. It may be a simple matter of twisted thinking and not selfishness.

As you can see in this story, wounded people wound people. When we are offended by someone, it's because we are focused on ourselves and are not looking behind the face. We are hearing **their thoughts** and when offended, we are giving place for the enemy to destroy our lives. Remember, you are in a war against a spiritual enemy. People are not your enemy.

Isn't that what criticism and judging is all about? "I am not happy with you because you didn't do it the way that I thought you should have." "You didn't respond to me the way you could have." It comes down to unfulfilled expectations to my way of thinking. The real problem is **me**. It's all about me. We have a mindset which centers around what I think to be true and what I think to be false, and there is no way but the highway. Unfortunately, love and mercy are not found in the mix.

Without God we cannot possibly love people for who God created them to be. We are all different. Our personalities are as different as the many ways that we perceive things. God delights in variety. Personally, I am very glad!

One day, a 21 year old man walked into our church. It was a mystery to me how he picked that church, because his home was on the other side of Baltimore and our small church was hidden from the main traffic. He was a hippie with ragged bell bottom jeans and old shoes that looked a mile too big. Long unruly hair, unshaven face and a shirt too big. He had a jacket that the men in the church had decided, and were absolutely certain was a state trooper's jacket that he surely had stolen! He smoked more than just cigarettes and so he smelled like tobacco and incense. Oh my! His presence caused quite an uprising. He sat on the back row and everyone moved away from him. Parents told their teenagers not to talk to him. Their strategy was "that if they ignored him, he would not come back." Eventually that worked.

We are called to demonstrate the love of the Father.

It was the height of the Jesus movement. Although being a hippie wannabe, I was constrained by the fear of my father. Instantly, I found this young man to be pleasant and interesting. I always favored the underdog, so I befriended him. Soon I learned that he lived with his mom who struggled in abject poverty and they lived in government housing that needed attention. Neither knew where his father was. She drank and he smoked. Both were terribly wounded people. As a product of his environment he had been abandoned and severely wounded. He was looking to find hope and someone to love him. Being skinny as a rail and not military material, the military refused him. There were no financial means for college. The elders and the congregation feared what they didn't understand and so they completely missed the opportunity to demonstrate the love of God. Instead of practicing James 2, "they dishonored the poor man, and made distinctions among themselves, and actually blasphemed the name by which they were called." By their words and their deeds, they judged him as unworthy to have in their worship service, in every sense of the word. Finally they ran him off. Imagine for a moment what that must have felt like. He came to a people, where the spirit of hope and love were supposed to be and did not find it there. He left more rejected, disappointed and wounded than when he came. Won't it be sad words to hear one day, "I sent someone to you, but you did not love him." It reminds me of the verse, John 1:11 "He came to His own, and those who were His own did not receive Him." Or, Hebrews 13:2 "Do not neglect to show hospitality to strangers, for by this some have entertained angels without knowing it."

We are called to be the love of Christ on the earth and manifest His Glory. God is looking for containers that He can dwell in that He might manifest His goodness through. The spirit of offense will stop us from being able to manifest His love to a broken and lost world, but only **if we allow it!**

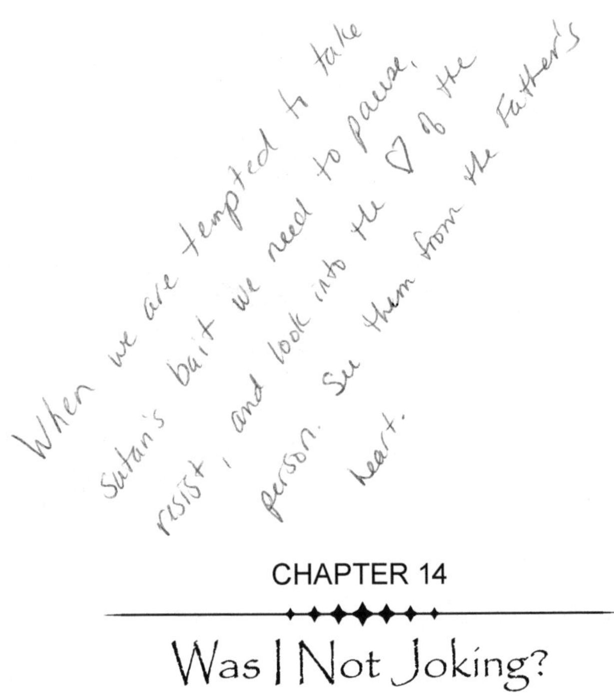

CHAPTER 14

Was I Not Joking?

John 12:32 “And I, if I am lifted up from the earth, will draw all men to Myself.” We lift Him up by allowing Love to flow through us.

Hebrews 1:3 says Jesus was the exact representation of the Father. We are suppose to be the exact representation of Christ. He is Love and we are suppose to be Love. When we are tempted to take satan’s bait we need to pause, resist, and look into the heart of the person. See them from the Father’s heart. If it is someone that you know and have relationship with, weigh what you hear by their character. Is this normal behavior for them? Many times we perceive what they say differently than how they actually meant it. So many arguments begin because of misperceptions. Men and women do not think alike. Often, my husband has given me instructions and when I get finished, I learn my interpretations was entirely different than his intentions.

"Father, forgive them. They know not what they do."

However, the enemy can also cause you to hear something entirely different than what was actually said. This is where we remember their character and who they really are. If their character is something that God is working on then love them. If their character is lacking then love them and continue to pray for them. God is faithful! The last words of Jesus, as he hung suspended on a cross for us, was "Father, forgive them. They know not what they do."

A written sentence has no inflection or tone that can be heard. And because of that, words have wounded many people on social media. Be very cautious what you write and what you say because you **will** be accountable. The scripture says that we will be accountable for every careless word. The Greek phrase is rema argos, meaning careless or inactive or unprofitable. We have been very careless with our words and are now seeing the results. In other words, "speak life, not death!" Do not even give the enemy opportunity by thinking death! It will go down to recesses of your heart and eventually it come out of your mouth! Neither should you be foolish and speak things against yourself like, "I think I am getting Alzheimer's" or "I am working on a stomach ulcer" or "I am such a meat head! Ha ha ha....." You will be sure to see those things manifest.

Ephesians 5:4 "and there must be no filthiness and silly talk, or coarse jesting, which are not fitting, but rather giving of thanks."

My heart is grieved when I hear **joking or jesting**. Through the years I have witnessed the great damage done through joking. I have heard jokes about fat ladies from the pulpit. How does that make women feel who struggle with their weight? Young or old. We live in a world where very skinny people think they are fat. The world is constantly pushing images at us that say, "you are not enough." What people need to hear is, God says, "you are perfect, beautiful and My delight!" People make light of their spouses. Parents embarrass their children. I shudder when I hear a Christian brother make light of another brother's hair loss. I realize that it is not a sensitive issue to all but it is to so many. Although the intentions were to direct that comment to one person, everyone in the room who struggles with hair loss, or fears it gets a ping (a seed) from the enemy. What are we thinking? If our child said something like that about another child, we would scold them!

We have a saying in our home. "Funny is for two people, not one." Comments about someone's color, or nationality, size, age or how they look, should never ever be in the Body of Christ. It is bad enough that the world does it, but it should never happen among

God's children. We never read where Jesus made a joke about how someone looked. As God's children, why would we? You might say, "Well it's just joking around. You are too serious." Oh really?

Proverbs 26:18-19 Like a madman who throws firebrands, arrows and death, so is the man who deceives his neighbor, and says, "Was I not joking?"

Proverbs 18:7 "A fool's mouth is his ruin, and his lips are the snare of his soul."

Proverbs 17:28 "Even a fool, when he keeps silent, is considered wise; when he closes his lips, he is considered prudent."

We are to build one another up, and not be the source of their stumbling.

We are to build one another up and stay away from anything that can cause our brother or sister to stumble. Be imitators of Christ and keep your **speech** and your **thoughts** pure.

Ephesians 4:29-30 "Let no unwholesome word proceed from your mouth, but only such a word as is good for edification according to the need of the moment, so that it will give grace to those who hear."

Proverbs 21:23 "He who guards his mouth and his tongue, guards his soul from trouble."

1 Corinthians 8:9 “But take care lest this liberty of yours somehow become a stumbling block to the weak.”

Keep in mind angels carry out our words. We may joke baldy today, and find ourselves baldy tomorrow. Hmmmmm..... We need to ask ourselves if we were the fat lady or the balding man, how would we like to be joked about in that manner? I knew a young lady who had beautiful penmanship. Actually quite gifted and extraordinary. One day she mocked about someone that she knew who was not blessed in the same way. Shortly after that, her beautiful penmanship was no longer available to her and to this day, it has not been restored. I know about many situations like this.

Matthew 7:2 “Do not judge lest you be judged. For in the way you judge, you will be judged; and by your standard of measure, it will be measured to you.” The Greek word for judge is diakrino, and it means to distinguish; discern one thing from another. It does not mean to criticize and condemn. If we criticize and condemn, we **will be** criticized and condemned. The same way that we measure out to others, we will be measured by that same standard of measure. This is a seed, time and harvest application. If the standard that we measure by is love, love is what we will get. If our standard of measure is that of gossip, we will be gossiped about. If our standard of measure is making jokes about someone’s bald head, we **will** find ourselves being the object of someone’s jokes one day.

We are, at the end of the day, how we treat one another.

We are, at the end of the day, how we treat one another. It may have been okay the first two times that we joked about someone's hair loss. However, we don't know what silent war rages against him bringing him to the point that his spirit has been weakened. The third time might just be too much for him. It is important to keep in mind that the enemy is continually setting the stage for hurt, and we do not want to assist the enemy in creating a broken heart. We say our cute comment and it's over for us. Forgotten. We go on about our day. However, the seeds have been planted and the enemy works diligently to destroy him. With the determination to bring more destruction, the enemy replays the comment over and over. We, who have been blessed to keep our hair, might ask the bald person if he would like to have hair instead of being bald. I can tell you that he would love to have a whole head of hair. Instead of joking about it, we should pray for his miracle! We allow ourselves to become a tool in the enemy's hand, carrying out the enemy's scheme. Our problem is that we really do not believe what the Word of God says about **our words**, nor do we **see** as the Father sees. We actually believe as the world believes, and that is "our words are no big deal." Our Father is Love. He does not make light of skinny, overweight or bald. If a person is going bald, it's because the enemy has stolen his hair, and it is a part of the devil's plan of internal destruction. It is important to guard our mouth, season our words, and keep sober. Be vigilant. The enemy seeks whom he may devour.

Years ago, I fell on my back and the doctor prescribed physical therapy. My muscles had started to atrophy. The physical therapist was a young woman in her twenties. She was a little overweight, but not obese. As she would bend me and work my muscles, she would say degrading, negative jokes about herself. One day I asked her, "Why do you say such terrible things about yourself?" I will never forget her response. She replied, "I just say it before anyone else does." Her self esteem had been so grievously damaged, she cursed herself all day long. Every time those words went out into the atmosphere, spiritual destruction was working. That is torment. I didn't know then, the things that I know now or I could have spoken life into her.

Lately the message of the Holy Spirit has been about **identity**. The reason that we curse ourselves and others, is we don't know who we are in Christ and we continue to make ourselves the perfect target for the spirit of offense. Understanding our identity is vitally important in overcoming the enemy. When we understand our royal status and our spiritual position in the Kingdom, we will be able to remind the devil, that it is we who have the authority. Satan is not to be ruler over us. We have dominion over him. The problem is we have completely overlooked the blood of Jesus, the power of the cross and the benefits of our salvation. The lack of intimacy with the Father gives the enemy opportunity to attack us. Through weakness in our spirit, our own words, and the sin of offense, he is able to rule over us. If you observe the Body of Christ, we are slipping and falling like walking on banana peels thrown on an iced over pond! We have not spent enough time with our Father God to learn what we were created to be. When we have someone that has hurt us and we refuse to forgive them, we will walk in darkness. However, if we are the one who offends without caring, it's because we haven't yet realized who we are in Christ. We were created for love and to **be love.**

John 3:19-20 "And this is the judgment, that the light (Jesus) has come into the world, and men loved the darkness rather than the light, for their deeds were evil. For everyone who does evil hates the light, and does not come to the light, lest his deeds will be exposed."

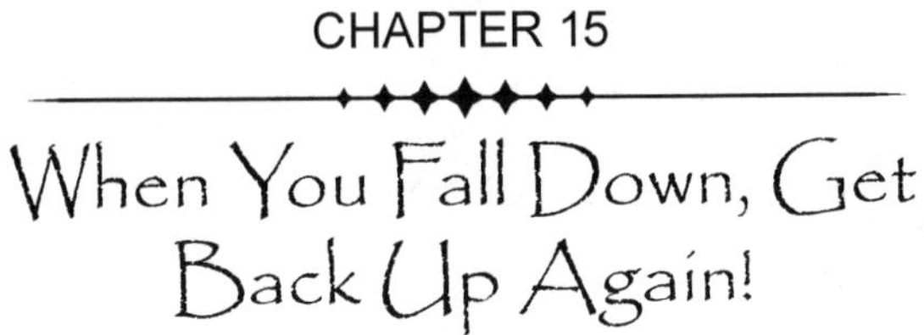

CHAPTER 15

When You Fall Down, Get Back Up Again!

When we get a clear revelation of what Jesus Christ has done in our behalf and what He has in His mind towards us, we will gladly give up unforgiveness in order to receive His fullness.

Jesus left the throne of Heaven and came for a people who **were not**, to make them a people who **could** be. He came to give acceptance to the rejected, love to the unloved, to bring a Father to the orphan, healing to the the broken, to be the food for the hungry and unsatisfied, and embrace the one that no one else wanted. He came for you and for me that we might know the Father personally and come to know how good He really is. Jesus came to take back what the enemy had stolen in the Garden in order to bring sons and daughters to a loving Father. He paid a very high price for redemption so He could release those held as prisoners in invisible prisons held as slaves to a harsh taskmaster.

The evil taskmaster steadily works on his plan of destruction by building on unforgiveness. Every wound we suffer becomes another bar in our prison cell, and the demons are there to torment at every opportunity. Soon the bars are so thick and close together that we can no longer **see** right from wrong. In fact, we can no longer see at all. Until we repent, it is dark in there and we have become desensitized to what is real and has been made available to us. We only see hopelessness, problems too big for us and a tangible loneliness mixed with despair. The prisoner becomes the object of satan's perverted entertainment.

Freedom is only as far as a cry for forgiveness.

However, there is a Great King who already made a public display of him! Hallelujah! Freedom is only as far as a cry for forgiveness!

Colossians 1:15 "And He is the image of the invisible God, the first born of all creation." We are to be the image of His Son, a walking testimony of the Father's heart to a lost and dying world. However, sometimes we slip and fall. When we do fall, we get back up again. If you have watched a toddler learning to walk they fall down and in a determination that they don't have to know what to call it, they get right back up and try again.

Proverbs 24:16 "For a righteous man falls seven times, and rises again,..." We do fall, but we get back up, dust ourselves off, and keep going. As we grow, we no longer find ourselves on the ground more than we see ourselves moving forward. Neither do we condemn ourselves, and hold unforgiveness towards ourselves. It is vitally important that we forgive ourselves, as well as we forgive others! Unforgiveness is torment, no matter who it is directed at.

Several years ago I went to a local chain pharmacy to get a prescription filled. Ten minutes after leaving the store, I noticed the price was three times higher than the pharmacy we normally use. I returned to the store to have it corrected and respectfully suggested that they had made a mistake. Their response was disinterested and not at all accommodating. It was a "tough luck, too bad for you, not budging" response. Nothing moved them. Unfortunately I was feeling seriously squeezed and Jesus was not what was about to come out. It seemed best to leave. Walking towards the front of the store, as the automatic door opened, I had a thought. It was another snare of the enemy but I wasn't at all in the Spirit at that moment. I thought, "I am going to voice my displeasure and tell them that this was not the way to do good business. (I know...) It was a moment of spiritual blindness and it did not go well. They were as apathetic as the first time and I was becoming increasingly distressed. As I approached the front to leave, an employee asked if I needed some help. I told her "No, thank you, I have been mistreated and am never coming back!" Oh, it was awful. A splendid display of unrighteousness! Now I had involved an innocent employee with a customer watching! Truly, I lost my head, meaning, it was a hostile takeover once I took the bait. It was devastating to me. When I got back to our shop, my husband just stood staring at me in disbelief. He said, "This is not like you! Why would you go back?" I said, "It was the principal of the thing!" Oops! Whenever you hear yourself say "it's the principal of the thing," unstop your spiritual ears. You have moved into a place called "it's about my rights!" For me, this was a mess up of monumental proportions! Once that came out of my mouth the Holy Spirit was able to break through to bring conviction. But we must always be certain that our conviction doesn't evolve into condemnation.

Listen, laugh, and then rejoice!

As I sat before my Father I heard "REJOICE!" I said, "are You kidding me!? Look at my behavior! I am so sorry!" He said, "I want you to learn to LAUGH, LISTEN, then REJOICE! Laugh in the face of the trial! Laugh at the enemy's attempt to stump you up. Laugh because I AM about to do a good thing for you. Then listen to what I AM saying through the clammer. Listen for My instruction. Listen because I AM present and ready to intercede in your behalf. Lastly I want you to rejoice because something that was meant to throw you off course is about to push you higher! Rejoice because the victory was set in place before the trial started. Rejoice because I love you that much! Rejoice, sing and dance because Greatness has come to show Himself mighty! Rejoice over the opportunity for someone to see Jesus where they might not have otherwise. Rejoice because it is your opportunity to shine as LOVE!"

This is an incredibly powerful revelation when we can grasp it. If we will put this revelation into demonstration we will overcome in the trial and will not submit to the spirit of offense. That spirit has set itself against you to destroy you. But "the battle belongs to the Lord!" Hallelujah! If we determine with our will to allow God to defend us, we will find the victory is already ours. Our victory was made available and set in place before the trial began! His grace is more than enough. When we are all about Him, He is all about us! His thoughts outnumber the sands of the seas! That's amazing since they are all good thoughts.

Psalms 139:17-18 "How precious also are Your thoughts to me, O God! How vast is the sum of them! If I should count them, they would outnumber the sand. When I awake, I am still with You."

His thoughts about you cannot be numbered. When Jesus looks at His hands and feet, He thinks about you. Scripture tells us that our names on inscribed in the palms of His hands.

This gives us a mental picture of just how much He loves us. His thoughts about me outnumber the sand. Isn't it interesting that God chose this analogy to describe His thoughts towards us?

One grain of sand is 0.01x 0.01x 0.01 inches cubed.
You could line up 100 grains of sand and
they would be 1 inch long.

Then 1,000,000 grains of sand would fit in one cubic inch (100^3).

1,000,000 x 12^3 = 1.728 billion grains of sand per cubic foot.

1.728 billion * 27 = 46.7 billion grains of sand per cubic yard.

So there are approximately 46.7 billion grains of sand per cubic yard of beach.

One cubic yard is only 36" deep and 36" by 36" wide. How many cubic yards are there in the beach? How many yards deep does it go? He is doing a lot of thinking about you! Isn't it sad that man can go through his day, and not think of Him at all? He waits for us to visit with Him.

Isaiah 55:8-9. "For My thoughts are not your thoughts, neither are your ways My ways," declares the LORD. "For as the heavens are higher than the earth, So are My ways higher than your ways and My thoughts than your thoughts."

CHAPTER 16

Resonating With the Heart of the Father

Our thoughts will resonate the sound of its source. Therefore, we want to have our thoughts come through the Holy Spirit. If we are to be the reflection of Jesus, as Jesus is the reflection of the Father, then our thoughts should resonate with the Father's heart. As our thought life resonates with the sound of Heaven, forgiveness is a natural response because offense cannot penetrate that atmosphere without our permission.

Our thoughts should resonate with the heart of Father.

I have asked permission to share a testimony about an amazing young woman and her struggles. Although she said that it was okay to print her name, she will remain nameless to honor the people involved. I will call her Julia. When I am reminded of her, I am humbled by the power of God and what He can do through us when our hearts are pliable to His will.

God had told me, "My Daughters have been going around the same mountain for years, and I want you to teach them how to walk in victory." So we meet twice a month and we learn how to walk in the dirty here and now. Out of this Bible study I have been privileged to watch God form a Gideon army of women who are growing strong in their faith, overcoming life's difficult circumstances and learning what it means to **be** Jesus wherever they go. You cannot imagine what a privilege it is to watch them as they grow. They humble me and make me hungry for more!

One Tuesday night, a young woman came. She had heard about the bible study. When she came in, she asked if she could stay. Because we have not known what we should know, we mistake brokenness for meekness. She sat and listened intently and left. Two weeks later, I received an email from her. The day she came, she had found out her husband had an affair, and the adulteress woman had his baby. This beautiful amazing young woman was broken to the point, she thought about killing herself. I don't know what pricked her heart, but she decided to give her life to God. In her email she wrote, "I had thoughts about killing myself, but now I have so much joy!" God replaced her bitterness with joy. He confirmed His love with a miracle. She wrote, "the next day I had hospital bill problems,

I prayed and prayed and after $4,500.00 that I owed, my total came down to $250! My insurance company had told me "sorry we can't help" but I called hospital and they said "your insurance covered the full percent". She continued, "no, there's no way because they told me they weren't going to help!" God was there with me the whole way! I was not a believer but now I am! Thank u God & u too Mrs Anita. I couldn't of done it alone! Slowly I will grow!! I love it! I love my life and I'm full of joy AGAIN!" (I have written it as I received it, because her heart was simple and so pure.)

This was an email which marks your heart for a lifetime. Julia saw the difference in **asking Jesus into her heart**, verses **giving her life to Jesus.** The Scripture does not say we are to 'give our heart to Jesus'. We give Him our life! It says, "to love Him with all your heart, mind, soul and strength." Julia took it seriously. To see a life like this changed is worth everything that you could possibly invest. However, Julia's story does not end there. God placed such a heart of forgiveness in her! She forgave her common law husband but before you gasp, know her story is not over. God put a heart of forgiveness in her for the mistress. Every Friday night when she gets off work, she goes to pick up the child in order for her husband to be able to spend time with his son. She sees the need for them to know one another. At the same time she ministers to the needs of the mistress, having a genuine desire for her to know the Jesus that she has found. This also gives the mother of the child, time for herself. Although the mother of the child is abusive, angry and hateful towards her, Julia is determined to show love towards the mistress in spite of her behavior. Little by little, she sees a glimmer. She loves the child and cares for him until she returns him to his mother on Sunday night. Who can do these things except through the Spirit of God? Every weekend is a test of faith. The common law husband? Her husband witnessed the mercy of God. He has seen such a change in her. He now attends church. They drive two hours from their home to go to church in Dallas. One particular Sunday when the invitation was given, he passed her up going to the altar. After church he told her they need to be married because he now sees that they live in fornication. They have just been married! Is anything too difficult for God?

It is amazing to see how quickly Julia is blooming. She is learning through a love affair with Jesus, just what God can do! She is learning to **be** Jesus and not simply **do** works. Those who simply do the works without being, could never truly love their husband's mistress and child. It takes the power of the Holy Spirit to forgive this kind of debt and take it to another level! She is learning to love her "neighbor as herself!"

Love is not a feeling.
Love is a person,.... it's Jesus.

I have named her story, the second greatest story ever told. It's the perfect representation of the heart of the Father. Although she has ***taken the hill***, she has to **maintain** love in order to keep it. She cannot take a vacation from being Love. The enemy is trying every scheme against her. God has done so much in her already but she is not a finished work yet! We are expecting great things! Though the enemy pushes at her every moment of every day, she has made a decision to choose "love" in order to please her Father.

If we hope to see God work through us in power then we ought to walk like He calls us to walk. In unity and love. Love is not a feeling. Love is a person! Our assignment from God is to love one another and demonstrate His love so those who see it may rejoice and be glad in Him. We cannot walk in unity and love if we give in to the spirit of offense.

There are people who suffer from what is commonly known as a **stronghold of rejection**. The term has been used as a shotgun approach to spiritual bondage like Alzheimer has been to various forms of senility. This term, stronghold of rejection is in actuality, repeated offenses which were successfully played out by the demonic and given ground through **meditation**. Offenses that were overlooked opportunities to love, forgive and bless. Some people are repeatedly offended. Jesus told us, "offenses will come" however we see people who are repeatedly offended. Why? The reason is because the enemy knows them well. He knows he can send an offense their way and they will meditate on it, instead of rejecting his scheme by making a choice to love and forgive.

The definition of rejection is "the act of throwing away; the act of casting off or forsaking; refusal to accept or grant." To a person who is easily hurt, every offense is seen as another example of being unaccepted. The word offend is "to cause dislike or anger; to pain, to annoy, to injure or disturb." These are not the same things. People will inadvertently offend someone by innocently overlooking them while their minds were elsewhere. Or perhaps they are having a bad day. They might answer abruptly because of the amount of stress they are under. This is not rejection. We have witnessed on many occasions, that things are not always as they appear. Life is busy for everyone and their actions and responses are not a matter of rejection.

As an example, I share the story of Alice whose name is changed in order to preserve dignity. She is nice looking, carries herself well and has a good job with influence, all of which people can find intimidating. Inside she is crippled by what she calls the stronghold of rejection. Alice said, "I have been hurt all my life. Person after person after person has rejected me. I have prayed to be delivered from this stronghold of rejection but God hasn't done it!" However, many of the things that she received as rejection were in actuality, setups of offense. If someone didn't call her on the phone, her response was

"I guess they don't want anything to do with me." In her mind she was being rejected. I would ask, "how often do you call them?" She had made no attempt to call or text them. Alice expected them to do something she herself had not done. If someone in a hurry failed to greet her, she took it as rejection. "I don't think they liked me." There were times that Alice would leave a message for someone to return her call and when she did not hear back from them, she would say, "I guess they don't want to help me. They are ignoring me." A week later she would tell me the person finally called and said, "the person could not return her call because they had experienced a tragedy." Unfortunately Alice meditated on the lies of the enemy for a week, until the enemy had built a strong case against the other person and against herself. Every time we fail to pass the tests of offense, we will get another opportunity to be offended. The enemy bringing offense after offense, attempts to add to a fortress of unforgiveness. Sadly, for some people, it never ends. It doesn't have to be like this. We are looking for God to deliver us from something He has already given us authority over.

When the enemy sees his plan worked and he has her undivided attention through meditation, dejection settles in. Dejection is depression of mind and lowness of spirit. If someone negligently and unknowingly offends her, it sends her into a tailspin of hurt, depression and withdraw. Not very long after, anger emerges. Out of the treasure chest in her heart, she drags out the skeletons of past offenses. That anger is unleashed on those closest to her.

What we have labeled as rejection, is unforgiven offenses.

What we have labeled as rejection for so many years, is unforgiven offenses. Offenses which have been held in account. "Love does not keep an account of a wrong suffered." When a bank account has had every penny withdrawn from it, no one goes back to withdraw funds because they know that there is nothing there to withdraw.

For many years, we have heard Christians say, "I have been praying that God would remove this rejection from me." Jesus paid a very high price that we could be free. To say that He hasn't delivered me, is contrary to the Word of God, making Him a liar.

2 Corinthians 5:17. "Therefore if anyone is in Christ, he is a new creature; the old things passed away; behold new things have come." He has already set us free. When we choose to meditate on past and current offenses, we create our own stumbling block.

We are our own stumbling block in our destiny.

In a case where Alice was innocently overlooked and not spoken to, who is actually guilty of sin? The person who was distracted? Or, Alice who listened to the voice of the enemy, and meditated on what she saw as offensive and became critical and judgmental which led to unforgiveness and separation? We are our own stumbling block in our destiny. Separation is a form of retaliation.

If we are in close intimate relationship with God, we can be poked with the hot iron of offense and Jesus will take the pain and the scar. When our minds are renewed with the Word of God, we will refuse to meditate on **any offense**. We make a choice to forgive the offender and love them as God loves them.

Acts 10:38 "You know of Jesus of Nazareth, how God anointed Him with the Holy Spirit and with power, and how He went about doing good and healing all who were oppressed by the devil, for God was with Him."

Jesus said that we will do greater things than He did. If we want to do just some of the things He did, we are going to have to walk in love. It does not matter what church group we attend or the big names we know or the people we hang with. The gifts we have been anointed with will not matter unless we walk in love with a pure heart.

CHAPTER 17

Where Is That Promised Power

The very first time that we are introduced to Gezahi, is in 2 Kings Chapter 4. Elisha had met the Shunammite woman and her husband. The woman told her husband she perceived that Elisha was a man of God. She asked her husband if they might build a room onto the house for the man of God. They built the room and whenever Elisha, the man of God, was passing through, he stayed at the couple's house. Elisha asked Gehazi to bring in the Shunammite woman and he asked the woman what he could do for her. And Gehazi answered, "Truly, she has no son and her husband is old." Gehazi not only was a witness to the miracle of the barren woman, but she had a child as was prophesied. He, also, witnessed something greater.

2 Kings 4:18-35 "When the child was grown, the day came that he went out to his father to the reapers. He said to his father, "My head, my head." And he said to his servant, "Carry him to his mother." When he had taken him and brought him to his mother, he sat on her lap until noon, and then died. She went up and laid him on the bed of the man of God, and shut the door behind him and went out. Then she called to her husband and said, "Please send me one of the servants and one of the donkeys, that I may run to the man of God and return." He said, "Why will you go to him today? It is neither new moon nor sabbath." And she said, "It will be well." Then she saddled a donkey and said to her servant, "Drive and go forward; do not slow down the pace for me unless I tell you." So she went and came to the man of God to Mount Carmel.

When the man of God saw her at a distance, he said to Gehazi his servant, "Behold, there is the Shunammite. "Please run now to meet her and say to her, 'Is it well with you? Is it well with your husband? Is it well with the child?'" And she answered, "It is well." When she came to the man of God to the hill, she caught hold of his feet. And Gehazi came near to push her away; but the man of God said, "Let her alone, for her soul is troubled within her; and the LORD has hidden it from me and has not told me." Then she said, "Did I ask for a son from my lord? Did I not say, 'Do not deceive me'?"

Then he said to Gehazi, "Gird up your loins and take my staff in your hand, and go your way; if you meet any man, do not salute him, and if anyone salutes you, do not answer him; and lay my staff on the lad's face." The mother of the lad said, "As the LORD lives and as you yourself live, I will not leave you." And he arose and followed her. Then Gehazi passed on before them and laid the staff on the lad's face, but there was no sound or response. So he returned to meet him and told him, "The lad has not awakened."

When Elisha came into the house, behold the lad was dead and laid on his bed. So he entered and shut the door behind them both and prayed to the LORD. And he went up and lay on the child, and put his mouth on his mouth and his eyes on his eyes and his hands on his hands, and he stretched himself on him; and the flesh of the child became warm. Then he returned and walked in the house once back and forth, and went up and stretched himself on him; and the lad sneezed seven times and the lad opened his eyes. He called Gehazi and said, "Call this Shunammite." So he called her. And when she came in to him, he said, "Take up your son." Then she went in and fell at his feet and bowed herself to the ground, and she took up her son and went out."

Gehazi was unable to raise the boy. What happened? The man of God told him exactly what to do. The scripture does say that Gehazi obeyed Elisha's instructions. When Elisha raised the boy, Gehazi witnessed another miracle.

Later Gerhazi witnessed still another miracle when there was pot of food with death in it and God restored it. He was hanging out with the well known man of God. It was an honor to be travel with Elisha and witness what God was doing!

2 Kings 5:1-14 "Now Naaman, captain of the army of the king of Aram, was a great man with his master, and highly respected, because by him the LORD had given victory to Aram. The man was also a valiant warrior, but he was a leper. Now the Arameans had gone out in bands and had taken captive a little girl from the land of Israel; and she waited on Naaman's wife. She said to her mistress, "I wish that my master were with the prophet who is in Samaria! Then he would cure him of his leprosy." Naaman went in and told his master, saying, "Thus and thus spoke the girl who is from the land of Israel." Then the king of Aram said, "Go now, and I will send a letter to the king of Israel." He departed and took with him ten talents of silver and six thousand shekels of gold and ten changes of clothes. He brought the letter to the king of Israel, saying, "And now as this letter comes to you, behold, I have sent Naaman my servant to you, that you may cure him of his leprosy." When the king of Israel read the letter, he tore his clothes and said, "Am I God, to kill and to make alive, that this man is sending word to me to cure a man of his leprosy? But consider now, and see how he is seeking a quarrel against me."

It happened when Elisha the man of God heard that the king of Israel had torn his clothes, that he sent word to the king, saying, "Why have you torn your clothes? Now let him come to me, and he shall know that there is a prophet in Israel." So Naaman came with his horses and his chariots and stood at the doorway of the house of Elisha. Elisha sent a messenger to him, saying, "Go and wash in the Jordan seven times, and your flesh will be restored to you and you will be clean." But Naaman was furious and went away and said, "Behold, I thought, 'He will surely come out to me and stand and call on the name of the LORD his God, and wave his hand over the place and cure the leper.' "Are not Abanah and Pharpar, the rivers of Damascus, better than all the waters of Israel? Could I not wash in them and be clean?" So he turned and went away in a rage. Then his servants came near and spoke to him and said, "My father, had the prophet told you to do some great thing, would you not have done it? How much more then, when he says to you, 'Wash, and be clean'?" So he went down and dipped himself seven times in the Jordan, according to the word of the man of God; and his flesh was restored like the flesh of a little child and he was clean."

Once again Gehazi witnessed a miracle. Not only was Naaman healed, but his skin was restored to that of a child. As Elisha trained under Elijah; so was Gehazi training under Elisha. Or was he?

Naaman returns to the man of God, and brings the silver, shekels of gold and the ten changes of clothes. However the man of God refuses his gifts of payment, so Naaman said, "If not, please let your servant at least be given two mules' load of earth; for your servant will no longer offer burnt offering nor will he sacrifice to other gods, but to the LORD." What? Two mules' load of earth, for what? It would be very much like you wanting to bless a man of God and offer him the five acre section you have so he can build his church to worship God. Elisha tells Naaman to go in peace.

2 Kings 5:20-27 "But Gehazi, the servant of Elisha the man of God, thought, "Behold, my master has spared this Naaman the Aramean, by not receiving from his hands what he brought. As the LORD lives, I will run after him and take something from him." So Gehazi pursued Naaman. When Naaman saw one running after him, he came down from the chariot to meet him and said, "Is all well?" He said, "All is well. My master has sent me, saying, 'Behold, just now two young men of the sons of the prophets have come to me from the hill country of Ephraim. Please give them a talent of silver and two changes of clothes.'" Naaman said, "Be pleased to take two talents." And he urged him, and bound two talents of silver in two bags with two changes of clothes and gave them to two of his servants; and they carried them before him. When he came to the hill, he took them from their hand and deposited them in the house, and he sent the men away, and they departed. But he went in and stood before his master. And Elisha said to him, "Where have you been, Gehazi?" And he said, "Your servant went nowhere."

Then he said to him, "Did not my heart go with you, when the man turned from his chariot to meet you? Is it a time to receive money and to receive clothes and olive groves and vineyards and sheep and oxen and male and female servants? "Therefore, the leprosy of Naaman shall cling to you and to your descendants forever." So he went out from his presence a leper as white as snow."

Gehazi had greed and deceit in his heart. The greed and the deceit kept him from walking in the power of God. It did not matter he hung out with the man of God. Even the power of association did not help him. We don't know how long greed and deceit were there, but we do know that as early as the Shunammite woman's son, he was not manifesting power, even when instructed what to do. It caused him to see with natural eyes and hear with natural ears. When sin is present, our ability to **see** is blocked. Like seeing in a mirror dimly. The many days that Elisha and Gehazi had traveled together, they would have talked. They experienced many things together. Yet, something entered into Gehazi's heart that manifested greed.

James 3:16 "For where jealousy and selfish ambition exist, there is disorder and every evil thing." Greed and deceit were operating in Gehazi, so we can know that it came from the root of jealousy and selfish ambition.

What is selfish ambition? It means to be self-seeking and always looking out for one's own interests above the interests of anyone else. The Greek word for selfish ambition is eritheia.

Those with selfish ambition are always thinking of how to put themselves forward without consideration to truth. Their attitude is make way for me! I am better than all of you, I deserve that. They may not ever speak it in words, but their fruit displays their heart.

In today's world, a selfish mindset and self seeking behavior is greatly applauded. We have all heard the saying "look out for number one." But the Bible considers selfish ambition as evil. It is one of the works of the flesh we read about in Galatians 5:20. In Romans 2:8 we read the wrath of God awaits those who are selfishly ambitious. In James 3:14-16 it says, the wisdom of a selfishly ambitious person comes from the devil, not from above. Paul's letter to the Philippians admonishes that even ministers of the gospel can be self-seeking and vainglorious (Phil. 1:17). He also warns us in Philippians 2:3-5, "Do nothing out of selfish ambition or vain conceit, but in humility consider others more better than yourselves. Each of you should look not only to your own interests but also to the interests of others. Your attitude should be the same as that of Christ Jesus." Where you see envy and strife, there is confusion and every evil deed.

In any case, we can know something caused Gehazi to be dissatisfied and wanting of more. He **lied** in order to obtain it from Naaman. Then released the servants from carrying it all the way to the house so he wouldn't be seen. Imagine, if it took two servants, each carrying a talent of silver, how heavy it was for Gehazi to carry both himself. Once there, he then hid it away so Elisha wouldn't know about it. Lastly, he lied to cover it all up, even though he knew that Elisha was a prophet and seer. Somewhere, at sometime, there was a separation in spirit, between the two. When there is a separation in spirit, it is because someone has been offended.

Mark 16:17-18 "And these signs will accompany those who have believed: in My name they will cast out demons, they will speak with new tongues; they will pick up serpents, and if they drink any deadly poison, it will not hurt them; they will lay hands on the sick, and they will recover."

We all want our prayers unhindered and answered. If we are a people who want to walk in the power and presence of God, we must learn to walk free of the spirit of offense. We have to walk soberly without taking the bait of offense.

The spirit of offense will cause us to do things and say things we normally would never do! Or react in a way we would not want others to see. This stops both the blessing and our promised power to do the works of God.

Isaiah 41:11-13. "Behold, all those who are angered at you will be shamed and dishonored; those who contend with you will be as nothing and will perish. You shall seek those who quarrel with you, but will not find them, those who war with you will be as nothing, and nonexistent. For I am the Lord your God, who upholds your right hand, who says to you, 'Do not fear, I will help you." God said if we get angry we will be shamed and dishonored. If we refuse to get offended, but choose to love, He will uphold us and help us.

CHAPTER 18

This Not My Fight!

Several years ago we lived in Kansas City, Missouri. We had purchased an air compressor which very soon after needed repair. It was under warranty and the only place that serviced them was in the area called Leeds. Leeds was so bad, the General Motors plant closed and moved out. There was only one store front left occupied in the entire block, and it was the repairman for the air compressor. My husband could not park in front of the shop and had to park just down a little ways. I sat in the truck while he got out to unload. Immediately, three enormous young men walk up to the truck. Their clothes were filthy and were unmistakably drug addicts. They proceeded to pour evil things from their mouths as they told my husband all the things they were going to do to me. I set in the front seat praying. Randy said, "I looked at each one of them in the eye." Then he turned his back to them. They stood high on the tall curb while Randy stood at a lower elevation in the street. As he waited to be physically assaulted he quietly prayed, "God, this is not my fight. This is Your fight!" When he turned back to look at them, he saw them running wildly as if they were being chased, (or they had just seen an angel bouncer). In the passenger door mirror, I could see only their backs as they took flight. Whatever they saw, they ran in terror.

The fight is not your fight, it is God's fight.

When you are being attacked, remember there are more with you than with them. The fight is not your fight, it's God's fight.

Proverbs 20:22 "Do not say, "I will repay evil"; wait for the Lord, and He will save you."

The problem has been when we are hurt or offended the enemy is there immediately to persuade us to serve judgement or retaliation for ourself. God said He will take care of the enemy. The offender is not the enemy. This cannot be said enough. However, when God does exercise vindication in our behalf, it is equally important we don't thrill at their outcome.

Proverbs 24:17. "Do not rejoice when your enemy falls, and do not let your heart be glad when he stumbles..."

Psalms 18:47 "The God who executes vengeance for me and subdues peoples under me; He delivers me from my enemies; surely Thou dost lift me up above those who rise against me; Thou dost rescue me from the violent man."

Psalms 35:1 "Contend, O Lord, with those who contend with me; fight against those who fight against me. Take hold of shield and buckler, and rise up for my help. Draw also the spear, and battle-axe to meet those who pursue me. Say to my soul, "I am your salvation."

1 Samuel 17:47 "And that all this assembly may know that the Lord does not deliver by sword or by spear; for the battle is the Lord's, and He will give you into our hands."

Isaiah 59:19 "So they will fear the name of the LORD from the west and His glory from the rising of the sun, for He will come like a rushing stream which the wind of the LORD drives."

When the enemy comes against us with all gusto and torment, the Spirit of the Lord will rise against him in our behalf if we will only walk in love. We won't have to defend ourself for **He is** our defense!

Isaiah 43:2. "When you pass through the waters, I will be with you; and through the rivers, they shall not overflow you. When you walk through the fire, you shall not be scorched, nor will the flame burn you."

We find ourselves in the fire and it feels like no one can understand our pain. However, we must keep our eyes fixed on Him and know He is Faithful to His promises. The Scripture says, "the waters would not overtake us, we would not be burned in the fire." Did you notice that He said, **not burned** as opposed to **not burned up!** The fire would not even scorch us. When I look back I realize when I felt overwhelmed, it was because I took my eyes off of Him and **looked at my circumstances.**

**Circumstances are not Truth.
Only the Word is Truth.**

Circumstances are not Truth! Only the Word is Truth. Circumstances lie and tell us there is no way out of this mess, but Truth says, "I AM God and there is no one like Me, Mighty to save, full of Lovingkindness and Mercy." Truth has a name! His name is Jesus!

Isaiah 45:2. "I will go before you and make the rough places smooth; I will shatter the doors of bronze and cut through their iron bars."

Deuteronomy 9:3 "Know therefore today that it is the Lord your God who is crossing over before you as a consuming fire. He will destroy them and He will subdue them before you; so that you may drive them out and destroy them quickly, just as the Lord has spoken to you."

2 Chronicles 32:7 "...for the one with us is greater than the one with him."

Isaiah 49:25. "... For I will contend with him who contends with you..."

Deuteronomy 33:27 "The eternal God is a dwelling place, and underneath are the everlasting arms; and He drove out the enemy from before you, and said, 'Destroy!'"

Jeremiah 1:8 "Do not be afraid of them, for I am with you to deliver you," says the Lord.

When we choose to follow God the enemy will do everything possible to push us back to make us quit. We will suffer persecution from him. Not from people, but from the powers of darkness as they operate through people. It is impossible to understand God's ways, unless we spend time with Him. Spending time with Him, builds up our immunity to what people think or say. Building up our **spiritual immunity** is to build up our **identity**. Our time spent with Him is not something that one can put a price on. How can we estimate a value for time spent in the presence of the One Who created Heaven and Earth and all that is in it? What can measure the benefits of entertaining The King? Is it possible to describe what joy there is in personally knowing the God who made us, keeps us, and then

'marries us'? Who can relate what joyful pleasure it is when we have refused to curse but gave a blessing instead? There are no words which can describe what it feels like to spend time with Him and have Him spend time with us. It is impossible to convey the emotions of what it is like when He comes to us unexpectedly, to love us at a "break into the day" moment.

CHAPTER 19

We Are The Beloved's, So Let's Run!

The Bride that Jesus is coming for is purely devoted, discerning in hearing His voice, skilled in warfare and eagerly anticipating her Bridegroom's arrival. She is no longer a babe but her spiritual eyesight has developed and recognizes the counterfeit. Every opportunity of offense serves as a stepping stone in her development of maturity. Love is her driving force and keeps her motivated with compassion. Her eyes are open to see. With every trial of offense she faces, **she can see the victory is in hand and brings with it greater authority**. The victory being set in place before the trial began, gives her an awareness of a new level of anointing and freedom. She has a revelation that the testing of her faith brings a new season of freshness and renewed strength for the next trial. This beautiful Bride is now using the opportunities of offense as exercise equipment to strengthen her spiritual character. The Bride of Christ is more than a conqueror. Her spiritual muscles are being trained to equip her with greater authority. A greater anointing in authority will be used to bring freedom to those around her. It's through these opportunities of offense, she takes what the enemy used to target her for destruction, and rises up out of the ashes into the manifested glory of her King. Miracles, dreams, and visions are now normal and expected.

Who is this victorious overcomer? Those of us who choose love, mercy and compassion instead of submitting to offense will position ourselves as that beautiful Bride of Christ. It's not too difficult for us. We can be like the Jesus in Julia. The promised power is made available to us as we submit to God, resist the devil, and see through the Father's heart.

In Your presence is fullness of joy.

Psalms 22:3 "Yet You are holy, O You who are enthroned upon the praises of Israel." God inhabits the praises of His people. Living a lifestyle in His presence is fullness of joy where everything is possible. Overcoming the spirit of offense is essential if we are to experience this fullness. Imagine trying to enter into His presence, going before this Great King in praise and worship, while you having offenses toward someone three rows to your left.

So that I was not distracted by the disinterest of others during the worship service, I would worship at the altar. It became another personal place of meeting. At the altar so many amazing things happen no one ever knows about except those who go there. I have been healed at the altar and seen many others healed there. One Sunday as I worshipped, the Holy Spirit was already moving. The last song was a lively one. Suddenly I unexpectedly had an open vision. Jesus was in front of me. He was on one bent knee at my feet and it took me by surprise. I stood staring. There on bended knee He lifted a ring to me and said, "Marry Me." Thoughts were reeling in my head. "Lord, You are kneeling, I should be at Your feet!" Again He said, "Marry Me." I said, "Yes! I want to marry You!" Then He bent down on two knees and began to wash my feet. I said, "Lord, I should wash Your feet!" Instantly my mortal fleshly mind had a question. I asked, "What are You washing my feet with?" He answered me, "Oil." In a moment the vision ended with the worship song. In my years of walking with the Lord, I can remember experiencing only a couple of open visions. As I started back to my seat I was in a daze and said, "What was that! Jesus, if that really was You, I have to know! Please confirm to me that this was You and not craziness!" I returned to my seat but before I could sit down, I noticed the pastor got up from his seat on the front row. He walked over, took the microphone and said, "I haven't thought of this song in so many years but I feel compelled to sing it right now." He sang, "Like oil upon your feet, like wine for you to drink, I pour my love on you...."

Jesus is coming for a bride who is not ashamed to love.

Some will mock and discard everything written. However, Jesus is coming for a Bride who is unashamed, passionate about Him, willing to love and forgive all, in spite of what others say and do. He is coming for a Bride who has reflected and manifested His love on the earth. Our works won't save us, our anointing won't keep us, our excuses won't justify us, and our good intentions won't deliver us. The only thing that will claim rights to our bridal gown will be **love from a pure heart, rich with forgiveness and a passion for our Bridegroom.**

Twelve years ago I had a dream which forever marked my life. It was about a king, a queen, and a son. It was time to select a wife for the son. They searched throughout the land and they chose me. I said, "I can't believe that they picked me. It must be a mistake! There are so many more worthy women!" Those assigned to the search took me to the castle. Once there they were going to prepare me to attend a special dinner. I was taken to a room where servants were told to get me ready. One of the servants brought a gown in while the queen was there waiting in the room with me. She approved the gown but never left the room and remained with me. The gown was white linen and very plain. No sequins, no pearls, no gathered fullness or fluff. I remember the gown had a high neck and long sleeves. They put the gown on me and I looked down. I could see my black bra from underneath. With disappointment I thought, "Oh no! I knew this would never work!" I was grieving with unbelief and reminding myself that I already knew that I couldn't possibly be the one. Thoughts were racing through my head wondering, "what in the world were they thinking when they chose me!" The moment I had the thought, the queen said, "Don't worry. We are going to take care of everything." Suddenly there was a knock on the door and the son stepped in. He stood looking at me with such indescribable love. I couldn't move or think. Time stood still. The love that came from him was like liquid going into the pores of my skin. Although he stood close enough to touch, I could not look into his face. The love was so tangible. (Then I woke.)

When I woke, I didn't want to move. The sensations of love in every pore of my skin was still there and I didn't want to lose that. However, I got up and went to the breakfast room and sat before Him. I could feel every pore on my body. I said to Him, "This dream needs no interpretation, Father. I understand that You were the king, the queen was the Holy Spirit, the son was Jesus, and the servants that had taken care of me were the angels. But are you saying something more? Is there something else?" He immediately responded, "I just wanted to give you a teeny hint of the taste of what Love feels like!" I call it the greatest chick flick of all times! The black bra? It represented my heart, but the Holy Spirit was saying, "We will take care of that, so no worries."

He didn't choose us because are good enough or lovely enough to make the grade. God chose us because He saw our value and our worth from afar and He wants us to see our value! Selected. Chosen. Prepared for Greatness, Himself. We will never see our value until we see the value in others. Neither will we see their value until we see the value that is in us. The Holy Spirit wants to take the black bra off of our heart and put on the robe of righteous thinking. White linen. Even that is scriptural.

What does God think about you? Unless you see with spiritual sight, you will not comprehend what His thoughts are towards you.

He says,

> I love you, my Child. I spread My mantle over you, as Boaz did cover Ruth. Like dew upon a blanket of rose petals, your beauty is ravishing. Your fragrance reaches My nostrils like an incense that no man has known or can describe. It's your love that delights Me. Your passion moves Me. My Beautiful Beautiful Bride. Your love causes Me to move Heaven in your behalf. Your steadiness is My joy. I AM keeping you, like that boulder set firmly in a river. Though the torrents press against you, I have you firmly set, firmly placed in position and the rushing waters 'will' go around you. You 'will not' be moved. I hold you. You, My Beloved

and Beautiful Beautiful Bride are a jewel in My crown, firmly appointed and set to shine for My Glory. You will 'not' fail. You won't fall short. You will 'not' slip. I hold to you tightly. As Boaz saw Ruth through eyes of delight, and set his heart to have her, so I too, delight to have you to call My own. I love you, as high as the Heavens are above the sea, without, measure. I AM holding you, so do not fear."

He will cause you to overcome the spirit of offense and He will deliver you from its hold. All you have to do is love Him enough to forgive those who have hurt you!

Revelations 12:11 says, "And they overcame him because of the blood of the Lamb, and because of the word of their testimony and they did not love their life even to death!" Our testimony will be that we loved Him passionately, and it spilled over into the lives of others. Unoffended and unashamed, laying down our lives and seeing Jesus glorified by His love flowing through us.

Now, run with your Lover through the fields of wheat, dance to the tune of His heart, and burn brightly that all may see, and say, "Great is their God, and greatly to be praised! Worthy is the Lamb!" Amen.

TESTIMONIES

The hurt, disappointment and grief I have personally experienced over the past year has been the most difficult period of my life. I allowed the "spirit of offense" I was receiving from a certain person to dictate my thoughts, moods and to some degree my actions. Anita's book clarified the cause, I was blinded from receiving God's word and promises by taking the "bait of offense" from the traps and temptations set by Satan through this person. As I have an analytical thought process, Anita told me very directly "the word of God is not meant for your mind, it is meant for your heart." As I read Anita's book, God put it on my heart to be proactive with love rather than reactive with anger to the "offenses" being received. God changing my heart protected me from taking the "bait of offense" from Satan's scheme and totally changed my reaction to the "offenses". Reacting with love in obedience to God's word rather than anger not only changed my inner peace and walk with God, it seemed to relieve some of the tension with this person whom I love unconditionally. I have no idea what God's plan is for me or the relationship, but I trust God's promise to have His will in both of our lives and I will wait for God's time, thank Him for it and rejoice in it. "Rejoice always, pray continually, give thanks in all circumstances; for this is God's will for you in Christ Jesus." As Anita has made it crystal clear, God neither wants or needs my help to change the heart of anyone. God sent this book and Anita's loving ministry to me at a time I desperately needed both. God is in charge and I will rest solely in God's favor when the "bait of offense" confronts me. "Do not be anxious about anything, but in every situation, by prayer and petition, with thanksgiving, present your requests to God. And the peace of God, which transcends all understanding, will guard your hearts and your minds in Christ Jesus." Congratulations Anita, you have served you Father well. Thank you and God Bless.

Michael

My journey of getting closer to God, has changed me in so many ways! I met Jesus through this teaching, and have given my life to be a daughter of The One True King. I have learned to love myself, and see myself through God's eyes for who I really am. In spite of what I deserved, and everyone's negative words, I learned who I am in Jesus Christ. My life has changed in so many ways. When God began changing me, he changed my husband. Now, my husband is going to church, and to a bible study!

Maggie

The last couple of months have been a challenge for me. There was a couple of things that happened in my life that I really thought I would have a hard time with but daily God gives me the strength to keep going. It is like he lifts me up, he has provided for my family and, in a time of need. He has given me the strength that I didn't think I had, and the peace that I never thought of having. My mother's health is doing much better. I see little things happen everyday and all I can say is "thank you Lord". I know He working in me, He is preparing me for something bigger and better, He is polishing me. I know that I don't walk alone and I am loving what I am feeling, I want to keep working on getting closer to him and be the woman He wants me to be. I don't have to be hurt or offended any more.

Joana

I been attending Mrs. Anita's Bible study for a little over a year and has gone over offense many times in the Bible. I started realizing I was being offended constantly by others around me. I started to realize who was really in control of my emotions and I knew with

God's help I would overcome it. I had been praying for my husband since he only attended church to make his family happy. He wasn't too sure of his beliefs and didn't really want to get involved n the church. I kept trying to change him and convince him but it was not working. We would constantly argue because I felt offended so I felt I had to respond back. Then when I realized I was getting offended by things my husband would say or did. I knew I had to seek God to help me not to be offended and not respond to the offense. I realized I was using the self pity card with God so when he did something I would feel sorry for myself and pray to God to help me. I realized self pity was not of God and I started catching myself whenever those thoughts started coming in to get them out and just start blessing my husband not for what I saw but what I wanted to see in him. Once I started to do that our relationship started to change and his attitude towards me changed. He went from being full of anger to being loving. He even just recently said he was going to attend a Men's Boot camp for our church which is a retreat for men to have a weekend without any distractions just God's presence. This was a shock to me never before would he have ever attended one of these things. He returned completely changed... you could sense it as he walked in the door. He told me he was going to make some changes in his life because he had accepted Jesus Christ into his life. Praise God an answered prayer.

Lettie

Offense is a very difficult feeling not to experience. I would feel offended at the snap of a finger. Today, people don't even realize it's a problem, you are have offense against the person and go about your business. Then little do you know, you start holding anger, resentment, un forgiveness, hatred etc. I didn't realize that offense was hurting my inner spirt man. It was stealing away my peace, blocking me from my blessings and not allowing me to walk in love. It was later brought to my attention that we must block offense completely by asking God for his help. No matter how much I wanted to not be offended. I would ask God to help guide me through. With meditation and prayer God began to break down the walls between people that had offended me in the past. I began to see them how God saw them. God sees people with love, he sees the best in all of us. My biggest issue, was not being angry toward my boss who repeatedly make me feel like I was not worthy. I meet a lady at church one night, who helped me to release all the anger and hurt I felt towards him. She suggested that I pray for him and ask God to bless him. I thought, "there is no way I want to pray for this man!" I finally gave in and begin praying for him, his wife, his health, and his business. I suddenly noticed all the problems, and all the tension was easing away. I kept on praying. I couldn't believe how fast it was working. God healed my heart through the prayers? I began to see him with love and I began to care for him. We ended up having a great friendship. A year later, he retired from his business and asked me if I wanted to purchase it from him. I was felt so honored! I felt so grateful to God because He blessed me through the storm. God simply wanted to teach me to love others. Behind the attitude, anger, and all the ugly he would express to me, God taught me to not take offense. He taught me to see people past the offense and He will take care of the rest.

Crystina

Thinking back to my divorce I can firmly say I tried to save my marriage more than I had ever tried to do anything in my life. My prayers were consistent, I prayed about any issues that prevented us from reconciling. I faithfully prayed the Word of God, and what He promises but my prayers was not answered. Not the way I wanted them to be. See, I learned that It wasn't that my prayer was not answered but my blessing was far beyond what I could SEE. God wanted to heal my heart, my hurt, my pain to use it for good. He is still preparing me, molding me into the person he wants me to be. He's healed my heart, he's working on me because I am his Beloved masterpiece. God is wonderful! I am learning who I am, and not to take offense.

Nadia

The teaching that exposes the "spirit of offense" is empowering; relaying "much needed to be read truth". It continues to be the most influential resource for our marriage, second to the word of God. We feel strongly that this should be required reading for all believers and nonbelievers. Moreover, for those in a committed relationship, this teaching should be mandatory reading as it was indeed instrumental in rescuing our marriage at a critical breaking point. We found that we were both guilty of offending the other more often than we realized, as well as being offended by the other. In addition, this awe-inspiring revelation brought to our attention not only our offenses towards one another, but how to resolve the root of the heart issue(s). We now implement this crucial study on a regular basis.

Anita's writing is anointed and does an excellent job at helping the reader identify offenses, and she also gives helpful ideas on how to disregard the spirit of offense and the spirit behind it. We devoured her writings from a perspective of two wounded and broken people that chose to marry the other.

This teaching lovingly convicted us, has brought us to repentance on numerous occasions, and changed the course our marriage so that God may be glorified!

Jeff & Stephanie Walker

Directors/ FFC Ministry

The subject of this book can be used as a tool to bring great victory in the lives of believers and non-believers. This is a Spirit anointed, Spirit inspired writing which impacted my personal life. The insight into the life of Joseph was a Rhema word for my personal life. Not allowing the spirit of offense is a big key to success in our walk with God, and man. As the author yielded to the Holy Spirit, the presentation is powerful and clear that this is the clear way to obtain freedom and complete increase in our lives.

James and Beverly Rackley

James Rackley Ministries

CONTACT INFORMATION

We hope that this book has blessed you and will be a tool that brings healing into your life.

It would be exciting to hear your testimony about what God is doing in your life through anything that you have gleaned from this book. Your testimony encourages others, which is what the "Body ministry" is all about.

You may contact us at propheticsignificance@gmail.com, or mail to:

Anita McCall

6813 Old Jacksonville Highway

Tyler, Texas 75703

“The Lord bless you, and keep you; The Lord make His face shine on you, and be gracious to you; The Lord lift up His countenance on you, and give you peace.”

Numbers 6:24-26

Made in the USA
Columbia, SC
30 September 2020

21833397R00124